BUSiN___

ReLoveution

A MINDSET PARADIGM FOR THE MODERN ENTREPRENEUR

TOBY McCARTNEY

Advance Praise for Business ReLOVEution

Warning! This book contains ideas that will change the world. As you read Toby's real-life stories and insightful reflections, you will realise that when you know why you want to make a difference, you will know what to do next. This book does not need to tell you how to become an entrepreneur, because a shift in attitude opens the doorway to your hidden talents and reveals new possibilities.

Vin Harris, Co-Founder and Trustee at Hart Knowe Trust

This book goes directly to the heart of why entrepreneurs often fail to achieve the success and freedom they want from running a business. Toby provides deep insight into the challenges we face, and proposes practical yet innovative solutions you can benefit from immediately.

Topher Morrison, CEO of Topher Communications

Mr. McCartney may not have picked up qualifications at school but he knows how to write a book. You will be gripped, and you will learn. Read this if you want to be a modern entrepreneur.

Emma Jones CBE, Founder, Enterprise Nation

Powerful, perceptive and practical advice from an author with a refreshing and highly entertaining perspective. Use this book and finally fulfil your purpose in the world!

Rich Soddy, Director and Co-Founder,
Sabadore Sports Marketing

Toby has written a truly 'must-have' guide for real people and modern entrepreneurs.

Its practical guidance and inspiring storytelling make the book both relatable and accessible. Toby's own personality consistently shines through, providing a guiding light to the journey. As an entrepreneur, he understands that being in business for yourself is not just about profit but purpose and humanity.

His masterful words clearly show us that a path into entrepreneurship is one of the greatest things we can do for ourselves and the planet.

Rob Love, CEO of Crowdfunder UK

A superb resource and must-read for any entrepreneur who wants practical yet innovative solutions that can be put into place immediately.

Robert Hokin, Managing Partner,
Greenbackers Investment Capital

This is a fantastic read by someone who speaks from experience as an entrepreneur who has chosen to do things differently, and succeeded! I really admire Toby, and recommend this book to anyone considering starting a business with a heart.

Emma MacLennan, Managing Director,
EASST Expertise Ltd

Editorial Project Management: Karen Rowe, karen@karenrowe.com

Cover Design: Kurt Richmond, kurt.richmond@oddballdesignz.com

Inside Layout: Ljiljana Pavkov

Printed in the United Kingdom

FIRST EDITION

ISBN: 978-1-8384391-0-1 (paperback)

ISBN: 978-1-8384391-1-8 (digital)

*To Kate, my beautiful, supportive
wife and soulmate, and my two girls,
India and Keira, who are already
disrupting the world for good.*

*"A ship in the harbour is safe, but
that is not what ships are built for."*

– John A. Shedd

TABLE OF

Contents

BUSINESS ReLoveution

Foreword

by James Timpson OBE

I KNOW A THING OR TWO ABOUT DISRUPTING BUSINESS. TIMPSON LTD. is a multi-national retailer specialising in shoe repairs, key cutting, locksmith services, dry cleaning and photo processing. It shouldn't exist and be successful but it does and it is.

While the business may have evolved since I became Chief Executive in 2002, the motivations and reasons for doing it remain the same. When the COVID-19 lockdown in March 2020 shuttered all of our 2100 retail locations, what saved us was our adherence to our core values. The company has been brutally impacted but I have been very careful to make sure that whilst everything else was changing around us, a number of things didn't change, which was our values and the culture of the company.

What I've tried to do is to keep reinforcing those values and the culture even when it was difficult. For example, we paid our colleagues 100% of their salary all the way through the furlough process, we kept our "Dreams Come True" scheme, birthdays off, bottles of champagne and did whatever was necessary to keep the business running. If we didn't have the values that we'd been feeding into the business for the last twenty years, we would have been in real trouble during this time. The kindness of our colleagues and customers has helped us stay positive during some very difficult days.

Organisations reflect the personalities of the people who run it. Which is why I think Toby McCartney's book on mindset paradigms is so timely. If you are about to embark on a new business, you need to know who you are, what you believe, what you are building and where you are going. There is more to running a business than making money – it's about values, culture and giving back. That is our focus at Timpson – and this book will help you make it yours as well.

In the future, I don't see how it will be possible to run a business without social purpose. You just can't. When you look at successful businesses that have run long-term, they have all invested in a strong culture with a strong set of values based on treating people as equals. They need people running the company who have clarity in leadership and purpose, so everyone knows what they are here to do. This book will help you do that. *Business ReLOVEution: A Mindset Paradigm for the Modern Entrepreneur* focuses on mindset strategies, tools for startups, small to medium-sized enterprises and socially responsible, environmental businesses like MacRebur Plastic Roads.

If I were starting out in business today, the one thing I'd want someone to tell me about leadership is what an amazing opportunity it is to inspire other people. My hope is that reading this book will encourage a few more entrepreneurs to challenge themselves not only to run a business, but to run a business with social purpose and to inspire others. *The future needs passionate, happy and confident leaders, willing to challenge the status quo and disrupt business for good.*

James Timpson OBE
Chief Executive of Timpson Ltd.

Negotiating with Russians

A BEAD OF COLD SWEAT RAN DOWN MY BACK AND I STARTED TO GET AN ITCHY feeling in my throat. The big guy across from me turned to his business partner, covered his mouth and whispered to him in Russian. (I don't speak Russian so the mouth-covering and the whispering weren't really necessary). The Russian looked at me and said in a calm and collected voice, 'We don't have the money here, but we can send someone to collect the £250,000 in cash. Will that work?'

I nearly pissed myself with fear.

I stared into space for a moment, and then explained that I needed a breath of fresh air. My colleagues and I stepped outside into the cold to discuss what to do next: this wasn't part of the script – we hadn't been trained for this. We were on business in Russia across the table from a company to whom we were trying to sell a £750,000 recycling factory. This was in the early days of MacRebur, a waste-plastics road-manufacturing company, and we were desperate to make this sale and return home with the good news to share with our investors. My colleagues and I work very differently: one is far more conservative than I will ever be, and the other far more maverick. We were torn. Can you imagine: £250,000 in cash?

On the other hand, how would we get it through customs? Also, it's not how business is done in our country. After a short debate and a lot of swearing, we decided not to take the cash but to ask for a bank deposit at a later date.

We went back into the room and sat opposite the Russians. I took a moment to push my breath into the bottom of my belly in order to keep my nerves at bay and said 'Thank you for your offer. We won't take the cash...' I paused, and then said 'But we will take diamonds if you have any!' My conservative colleague nearly fainted. The Russian laughed out loud, and we proceeded with the details of the bank draft so we could close the deal.

The Problem with Being an Entrepreneur

The point of this story is that it's not easy being an entrepreneur.

In fact, it is often really hard.

You are constantly struggling with your own ethical stance in life, your values are constantly being challenged and you have to make decisions you feel are completely outside your knowledge and skills base. Even if you are doing it right, you are often ridiculed by haters and made to look stupid by those who can't – or won't – see your vision. On a daily basis you can feel worthless and overwhelmed. If you are looking for self-worth and praise, then don't become an entrepreneur. It's certainly not a career for the fainthearted.

It's much easier getting a job and working for someone else. The problem is, most jobs – and most companies – suck! The majority of companies have managers with impressive CVs and scrolls' worth of qualifications who have learned old-school leadership and management techniques from old-school books and even older business school teachers. They have little or no experience of actually running a business or managing people themselves. You have to go far to find managers who truly understand the emotional beings who make up their staff.

The modern manager knows how to be a modern *leader*. They aim to inspire and motivate their employees while helping them grow and develop their skills.

This challenge doesn't just play out in large corporations. It's the same challenge faced by most *unmodern* entrepreneurs. It's especially prevalent in the lone entrepreneur with a sole member of staff: him or herself.

Management and leadership starts with management and leadership of ourselves. We have to master that before we can effectively manage and lead others.

Do Things Differently

There is good news though. I have solutions to the challenges – so if I haven't put you off, read on. My solutions aren't in many business books, but they are solutions I use every day to help keep myself on the right path. They are a collection of mindset techniques I believe every entrepreneur on the planet can use to keep themselves sane in the insane world of business.

One of my top values is trust, so let me be honest with you upfront. I don't have any school qualifications *at all*.

What I do have is more than two decades of real-world experience as an entrepreneur. I've spent my whole life looking for ways to disrupt, to break out of what is expected. Nowhere have I applied this principal more than in business. Whether it be through revolutionising how people book travel, starting a shoe company with a social ideal, producing a musical album for an amazing singer-songwriter

17

or developing the world's largest waste-plastics road-manufacturing company, my goal has been to do things differently.

I've sought to disrupt business norms for my entire career. I don't believe in putting on a fake show; I don't believe in trampling on others or on the planet in order to make money. I believe we can be more 'modern' entrepreneurs. To me, business is done through manners and rapport rather than through sales strategies and techniques. If a businessman or businesswoman learns sales strategies and techniques but doesn't have manners, they're not going to do as much modern business.

I've written this book to start an entrepreneurial revolution. One which involves a change of mindset to put a focus on an entrepreneur's values, identity and purpose, rather than on business models, financial planning and sales tactics.

I've always suffered with dyslexia, so when I came up with the title of this book I was thinking 'Business Revolution' but wrote down 'Business ReLOVEution'. Because I still struggle to learn the same way as others learn, and because the book is about an entrepreneur's mindset, my editor thought I had been pretty clever.

I kept the title and took the credit. So this book describes a business 'ReLOVEution'! It shows you how to love yourself and in turn love being a modern entrepreneur.

My goal is not to create a revolution of people who start businesses with the intention of disrupting rules and regulations or societal expectations for no other reason than 'sticking it to the man.' I wrote this book to encourage serious, sincere entrepreneurs to think outside the box. I want to help you resist the naysayers or the inner voices that say, 'You can't do that', so you instead say, 'Yes, I can'.

I didn't learn much at school, as I've already confessed, but I did learn one thing before I went into business: I learned how to be kind and compassionate, both to myself and towards others. That's the kind of lesson I want to share. I want to encourage you to disregard traditional ideas about business while sticking to this one simple rule: always seek to be a friend.

I want to help set you up for success by sharing modern mindset stories and strategies that will encourage you to find your own ways to 'negotiate with Russians'. You can do it in a way that benefits everyone. Whether it's a customer, client, spouse or child, a stranger or the whole planet: we all benefit when we disrupt business for good.

Right now, I'm being kind and compassionate towards you. That's why I should say that if you are looking for an academic education in business, then my book, my training programmes, my mastermind groups or any of my products and services, are probably not for you. But if you want to learn and change with tools and techniques that will really make a difference, and you can put up with my warped sense of humour, then stick with me.

There are a ton of books out there on business and entrepreneurship already, and if you are worth your salt as an entrepreneur, you've probably read many of them. This book doesn't seek to replace those books, but rather to enhance them by using personal stories (which I believe to be one of the best teaching tools out there) and mindset exercises (another of the most powerful tools my wife and I use in our training and coaching programmes).

I imagine you came to this book because you're thinking of starting a business, perhaps even your first. Or maybe you already have a small business and you want to take the next step in your journey as an entrepreneur. If you have been an employee your whole life, starting a business is going to require a disruption in your mindset, and if you already have a business, then growing it might require you to think outside the box.

This book is organised into twenty principles to aid the new entrepreneur in establishing a successful business that disrupts for good. Each chapter includes stories and anecdotes from my own experiences in business, and those of others. To reinforce the principles,

I've included mindset exercises – inspired by techniques I use with my clients – to encourage you to step outside your current habits and beliefs and see the bigger picture of who you are and what you (and your business) can become.

I want to inspire you to dream big and manifest even bigger.

So here we go… If I haven't put you off being entrepreneurial yet, then let's get started with learning how one becomes a modern entrepreneur.

CHAPTER ONE

Occasional Acts of Lunacy

'THE FUTURE DOES NOT BODE WELL FOR TOBY.'

That's what my A-level computing teacher wrote in my report at boarding school. Another wrote, 'A mixed term for Toby, in which his general good behaviour has been spoilt by occasional acts of lunacy.'

It would probably come as a huge surprise to my teachers that I'm not living under a bridge. They labelled me as 'thick'.

I wasn't thick. I had dyslexia.

Before I worked that out, though, I'd built up a load of limiting beliefs about being the person they told me I was.

Mr. Jones — I.T.

I was sent to boarding school when I was eight years old. I hated it. I disliked being away from my parents, who were in the military, and was bullied relentlessly by kids and even some of the teachers. I was never in class and I was often suspended. I didn't pass my exams because I didn't *believe* I could pass them.

I needed a way out of being the school punch bag, so I spoke to my grandfather, who I would often confide in and seek advice from. He was very good at woodwork, so he made me a tuck box, which boarding school kids use to keep food treats from home. It was a big wooden box with a lock, painted black, with my initials on the front.

At the beginning of each term, my grandfather took me to a super-store called Food Giant to buy chocolate bars, sweets and other goodies to fill my box. I wasn't really into sweets, but I'd worked out that other kids really loved them.

I used to wait until two weeks after the start of term, when all the other kids had eaten their sweets from home. Then I would unlock my tuck box. On the inside of the lid, I pasted a price list for each item.

Remember Red in *Shawshank Redemption*, the prisoner who can get everyone stuff?

I was the Red of Lime House School. I was the person who could get stuff.

That stopped me being bullied. It also gave me my first taste of being an entrepreneur.

Defining the Modern Entrepreneur

Most people have no idea what a modern entrepreneur really is.

The title 'entrepreneur' is bandied about too often by people who wouldn't recognise an entrepreneur if they were sold one.

Real entrepreneurs are a rare breed. You don't qualify as an entre-preneur if you have built a career in an industry and managed to save enough money to buy a second home that you rent out or if you sell some of your children's old toys on eBay to raise money to buy more toys this Christmas. You won't find many modern entrepreneurs in politics, finance, local authorities or the retail industry. They tend not to be interested in job titles or letters after their name, or to get their self-worth from directing staff in companies or large corporations.

The modern entrepreneur searches for innovation, purpose and freedom in all that they do. The restrictions that come with most nine–to–five jobs take all three of those qualities away.

Entrepreneurs are innovators. The modern entrepreneur brings ideas to life. Think of all the new technology and ideas that have come to life over the past few years. Those were all once just an idea – until an entrepreneur got involved.

Entrepreneurs have a purpose. The modern entrepreneur structures their business around a 'cause' worth fighting for but works out how to mix their purpose with profit. They understand that both purpose and profit are powerful 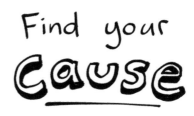 motivators for change, and gain support for their cause from others because of it.

Entrepreneurs are free. The best modern entrepreneurs can work out what tasks would be better done by someone more qualified or knowledgeable than themselves versus what tasks they *must* do themselves to keep their businesses earning more profit and thus scaling up their purpose. Setting aside any ego and firing yourself from tasks others could do more effectively is an essential modern entrepreneurial skill.

The traditional dictionary definition of an entrepreneur is: 'A person who sets up a business or businesses, taking on financial risks in the *hope of profit'*.

I've added the italics ... because today, there's much more to it than that. The modern entrepreneur doesn't simply live to make money and if they rely on *hope* alone, they will never make it.

Today, the values you're likely to hear linked to modern entrepreneurs are less to do with profitability and more to do with innovation, creativity, revolution and disruption. The modern entrepreneur understands that he or she must live by such values – but that doing so is not always easy.

Looking back at my tuck-shop business, I see that I had an innovative idea (sell sweets when everyone else had eaten theirs), I definitely had a purpose (stop being bullied) – and although the teachers might disagree, I was free.

Innovation, purpose, freedom. I was already a trainee modern entrepreneur.

Different Behaviours

There's a close link between having dyslexia and being an entrepreneur. According to a study by Julie Logan, a professor of Entrepreneurship at London's Cass Business School, 20% of UK entrepreneurs have dyslexia, and a staggering 35% in the United States. The US study followed up earlier research that revealed that UK entrepreneurs are five times more likely to suffer from dyslexia than the average UK citizen (4% of the general UK population is dyslexic). [1]

At university, by the way, I realised that I'm not dyslexic; instead, I 'have' dyslexia. It's a tiny change in words, but it generates a very different emotion. Dyslexia is not part of my identity. It's simply part of my behaviours. Who I am remains the same. It's important to separate the label of my behaviours from my identity. I believe that people are not their behaviours. Behaviours can be changed relatively easily and quickly, whereas one's core identity tends to be something you search for and work towards your whole life.

When I'm trying to learn something new through reading, I just have to change my behaviour by turning the subject into visual pictures. That learning strategy has enabled me to learn whatever I want.

That's why I've included 'doodles' throughout the book. They're part of my learning strategy. They help me, and I think they might help everyone else, too.

My business success wouldn't have been possible without my changed behaviours.

I'm different, I know that, but I embrace it: I hate the mundane or boring choices many people make. Being different comes naturally to me – in life, and in business. If something is being done the way it's always been done, I like to stir things up and do it differently.

In business, being different and having different products and solutions is beneficial. Business is built around being different – either by inventing something new, or by taking what already exists and making it better. What makes a business different is what the customer buys into.

It's much easier to go into a market that already exists and make it better than to try and create a new market from a new invention. Today, my wife and I run a successful training and coaching business. When we started the business some 20 years ago, there were a number of businesses promoting the same or similar products and services to ours. In order to carve out our own part of the market, we simply looked at what already existed, and made it better. We provided more benefits, a better service and a uniqueness that the other training schools didn't have. We used what existed as a benchmark to make our business better.

Some of the core principles from our coaching business are woven throughout this book in the form of mindset exercises: These are tools to help enhance the principles at the heart of each chapter. Each principle seeks to help the modern entrepreneur do one thing: succeed with purpose and love themselves.

***

In today's political climate, after COVID-19 forced many people to reinvent their lives and work and live remotely, it feels like now is the time to think differently.

Let's stop doing the same old crap we've always done.

Any business that is going to make it through these changing times should have either or both a social impact and an environmental impact.

You might as well stop reading now if you don't agree.

The truth is that customers are far smarter than ever before and their buying strategies are driven by their inner values and their beliefs. For the vast majority of people, those inner values include kindness and compassion. If a business can meet those values through demonstrating kindness and compassion to the environment, and kindness and compassion towards other people, it's much far more likely the business will thrive rather than just survive (or fail miserably).

If a drinks corporation were just starting out today, for example, it wouldn't be able to function within the traditional business model. It would have to think far more than previous companies in the market about its environmental impact – for example, by producing bottles from a recyclable glass or plastic or a compostable plastic.

Such changes are possible, though. Here are examples of businesses around the world that have figured out how to successfully incorporate environmental and social impacts into their business model:

- **Natura**, a Brazilian cosmetics company, guides product innovations that focus on preserving biodiversity and traditional knowledge and culture in Amazonia. Its Ekos products are sustainably sourced and biodegradable, and Natura has established agreements with each of its 2,500 small suppliers to guard against the unethical commercialisation of the region's genetic and cultural heritage.[2]

- **SC Johnson**, the world's leading maker of insect-control products, partnered with USAID and the Borlaug Institute of Texas A&M University to work with Rwandan farmers and their communities to sustainably farm the plants that supply pyrethrum, a key ingredient of their products. SC Johnson developed a bundle of insect-control products, ranging from repellents to home cleaning sprays, in refillable formats and marketed these products through clubs of seven or more homemakers, who also participated in group coaching sessions around home and family-care best practices. [3]

- **Interface**, the world's leading carpet tile manufacturer, uses plastics and polymers rather than bitumen-based materials for carpet backing, enabling carpets to be recycled and produce less waste. The company also tapes their tiles together, rather than gluing them down, avoiding the use of toxic chemicals.

- **Clif Bar** has embedded sustainability in its employee benefits package by including incentives for actions such as making eco-friendly home improvements and purchasing a fuel-efficient car. Employees are rewarded for such positive behaviour and recognised at year-end.

- From a social perspective, companies such as **Netflix** and **Spotify** offer benefits to support their employees and families. Netflix offers 52 weeks of paid parental leave, which can be taken at any time, whether it is the first year of the child's life or another time that suits their needs. This compares to 18 weeks at other tech companies. Spotify offers a similar programme, although for a shorter duration of 24 weeks of paid leave.

- **New Belgium Brewing Company** is owned entirely by its employees through a stock ownership plan focused on sustainability. Its Fort Collins brewery produces 18% of its own electricity through solar panels and wastewater. It also contributes to bicycle and eco-focused organisations. According to their Director of Social and Environmental Impact, Katie Wallace: 'We consider social and environmental well-being to be intricately intertwined'.

Socially and environmentally-focused businesses will attract the customers of the future. From London to New York and other large cities anywhere in the world, the businesses that really thrive are those that are producing a fair-trade food or a product that's not wrapped in single-use plastic but rather something recyclable. If businesses of the future miss out on this shift, then they're doomed.

Do your research, check out what other companies are doing – I bet my next deal money that the ones who make it into the press are either the businesses who have gone bust, or those with an environmental and social conscience.

We are no longer in an era where the main focus of business is capitalism. Take large corporations such as Amazon and Google, which do not pay taxes in the UK for their operations, instead opting to set up in Ireland, where tax is much lower. On one hand, this is clearly a smart business model because they save money – lots of money. On the other hand, such practices have provoked an entire group of people who will never shop at Amazon or Google, preferring their local suppliers to any online businesses.

Thanks at least in part to the internet, environmental and socially conscious businesses have a voice now! If that group continues to grow, and large businesses of the past and present lose enough of their customer base to cottage industries, then all businesses will be forced to change their values so that they incorporate social and environmental responsibility.

Disrupting Business for Good

One way to disrupt for good is to build a business with a social or environmental impact component, preferably from the very first business model rather than as an afterthought. *Start* by working out how to bend the rules. Ask yourself, 'How do I create a positive impact and leave a legacy?' The answer is not always obvious; in fact, it's rarely the obvious answers that make the biggest impact. It's not just about giving some of your profits to a charity. It's about answering the question, 'What's the core of my business? What legacy is this business going to create?'

To give you an example, I am the CEO of a company I co-founded called MacRebur Limited. We collect waste plastics, process them and use them to replace bitumen, the black oil used in surfacing roads. From the start, we had the environmental impact licked but not the social impact. So I created the MacRebur Foundation, which is designed around organising local litter pick-ups all over the world, from rivers and oceans to old schoolyards, from the beaches of Florida to the streets of Delhi.

We sponsor as many groups as we can. We provide high visibility shirts and hard hats, and grabbers so they don't have to touch the rubbish. Rather than sending that rubbish to a landfill, we buy it off them and use those non-recyclable plastics as part of our process. That's how we create the social side of our business: we bring local people together with a common sense of purpose. If people have a task they can do together, such as a local litter pick-up, it doesn't just help the local environment. It also makes a social impact on a person's life and creates connection and a sense of well-being.

Many other well-known businesses have followed this model. You might not have heard of John Paul DeJoria – but I bet you've heard of Paul Mitchell hair products and Patrón tequila. DeJoria founded both of these companies. DeJoria was homeless as a young adult, while parenting a two-year-old son, but he had a vision—and $700 in start-up cash. Today, he is a billionaire philanthropist who supports a number of social causes, including homelessness.

The lesson is that businesses do not have to choose between purpose and profit. Disrupting business for good is not an either/or proposition. You can have both. You may just need to think a little differently about how to do it.

With the MacRebur Foundation, for example, we are not only having an environmental and social impact. We are also creating a narrative we can publicise, so we get PR and marketing from our 'good' activities. It's a win-win for everyone.

If a business makes a customer's life better, a customer can't say no to it. It doesn't matter what you charge, because it's so much better than what they have now. And if you can make the business even better by being socially and environmentally different from other businesses, you've got a winner: you've created a lifetime business, not just a dalliance. Adding a social or environmental impact as part of a business's core is far better advertising than a Facebook advert or a Google pay-per-click spend.

Starting a business isn't just about disrupting and changing what currently exists to make something better. It can be about creating something new to solve a problem that no one else has been able to solve yet. If it's outside the box, some people may call your vision an 'act of lunacy'. Don't be afraid to do it anyway.

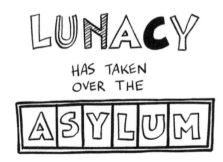

Mindset Exercise: Open Your Mind

It's pretty safe to say that you need to have an idea before you can get into the business of that idea, but often people spend days and months (and sometimes years) trying to come up with an idea that's innovative and revolutionary and world changing. A business idea doesn't have to be so grandiose. The idea, at the beginning anyway, might be small. It might seem ridiculous or insignificant, like my idea of putting waste plastics into roads rather than into landfill sites or oceans. A small, ridiculous and insignificant idea can become world-changing in the end.

Your initial idea is like the seed you plant in spring; as long as you nurture it, by the time you get to summer, you are cutting off the flowers and giving them to your neighbours because you have so many.

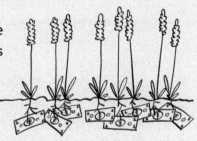

THE HARVEST

Start with just one seed. Ask yourself, 'What would I like to have happen?' If you could do anything—if you just said, 'Screw it, Let's Do IT', as the title of Richard Branson's book put it, what would that *IT* be? You have skills in some areas already: what could you do with them? What excites you? What motivates you? What idea could you create today that could be planted and grown into many other ideas?

Mindset Exercise: Business Lunch

This is an easy-to-use mindset technique to start practising mindfulness. It can be attempted by anyone with any kind of food and can be used to calm any nerves or anxiety when you are in business meetings or negotiations – or simply having your lunch with a client.

Here's how simple it can be to be mindful in the moment. When you have your lunch, or any food, in front of you, look at the detail of:

- How it looks
- How it feels if you can touch it
- How it changes when you cut it or stab it with your fork
- How it smells
- How it tastes

Focusing on these micro-details will bring your mind to the present, to what is right in front of you.

By focusing on your food and making a point to notice every detail about it you are unlikely to be using up any energy, time and attention on the stresses and anxieties of what might or might not be bothering you from whatever meeting or other situation you are in.

When you follow these instructions and take notice, it is much easier to focus on what is in front of you rather than on anything else. If your mind does wander back onto the old emotions, gently remind yourself of what you are focusing on in that moment, which is all totally in your control.

Chapter One Principle:

Be different.

Just Another Splinter in the Arse

I WAS SO SUCCESSFUL WITH MY TUCK-SHOP BUSINESS AT SCHOOL THAT I missed all of my lessons. While everyone else was in geography, history or maths, I was hiding around the corner waiting for them to come out.

I made a lot of money for a kid, but I left school without any qualifications. I failed every exam except biology – and I only passed that one because I knew all the answers to the questions about women's anatomy.

When my results came in, I dreaded having to tell my parents.

My father was a military man, and had been a soldier since the age of 16. He worked his way up the ranks to become a Captain in the army and this took real determination and grit to do. I was more interested in making money than climbing a ladder and I didn't have the guts to tell him that I had not been to the lessons he had been paying for.

'How did you do, son?' he asked.

I stood to attention and said, 'I'm really sorry, Dad, but I didn't pass anything.' (I didn't think he'd find my Biology result much compensation). I thought he would kill me. I had no idea what I was going to do with my life. Perhaps I could join the Foreign Legion.

He looked me square in the face and said, 'Well, son, this is just another splinter in the arse as you slide down the banister of life.'

Our relationship changed in that moment. It was the first time I'd seen my father as anything other than the military Captain of my life. He smiled back at me.

I've come back to that phrase again and again. When something, anything, doesn't go quite to plan, that's what I remind myself. It's another splinter in the arse as we slide down the banister of life. That's why I don't believe in failure. Instead, I believe in feedback. Some feedback, like splinters, just hurts a little more than others.

My dad continued, 'So, son, what are you going to do now? You haven't got any qualifications, so you can't go to university. You're going to have to get a job.'

Having to get a job was the worst thing I could think of. It was my greatest fear. I already knew I was not suited to taking orders from anyone. My dad, with his military background, issued orders all the time – but I wasn't designed to take them; only change them to suit myself.

I told him, 'I'm going to travel the world and see if I can find myself.' He took one look at me and said, 'Son, what if you find yourself … and he's a dickhead, too?'

Now *that* feedback soon made me realise that maybe travelling wasn't right for me. I wasn't likely to 'find myself' in Thailand, so I might as well look for myself at home while I figured out what to do next.

I did what I've always done best: I was myself. I phoned a university and talked my way into getting a place, even though I didn't have the grades. But I could speak to people in a way that made them become friends, and my new friend on the other end of the phone gave me a place, despite my obvious lack of qualifications.

I studied telecommunications engineering, which I only chose because my father was a telecoms engineer in The Royal Signals in the British Army, so I knew he could help with my studies. It took me six years to graduate – but I made it, graduating with a 2:1 Honours degree and letters to add to my name, (P.L.O.N.K.E.R).

My real education wasn't in the classroom, however. I soon drank my way through the £2,000 student loan I'd received and was faced with having to fund myself through the rest of my university life. I wasn't about to get a job – so I figured I'd start my own business.

Something had been born in me when I started my tuck box business at school. I wanted to be an entrepreneur. At nine years old, I wrote a letter to the entrepreneur I admired most and wanted to be like, Richard Branson (long before he became 'Sir' Richard). Would you believe it? He wrote back. I have the letter to this day. He had just started Virgin Atlantic, and I asked him what it was like to be in business and own an airline.

He wrote back to tell me what I needed to do in order to become an entrepreneur: stay in school and get good qualifications.

You already know I didn't take his advice – but I did keep the letter. And I've never stopped following his career or aspiring to be like him.

At university, I was lucky enough to have a good friend who was stupid enough to go into business with me. He had a bit more money than me as he was a 'mature' student who had worked before going to university. Not that there was much mature about either of us – even today. I got him to invest in the idea of creating a window-cleaning business, and gave him a list of things to buy from the local hardware shop: shammies, a bucket, some cloths and some window cleaning supplies.

Meanwhile, I worked on marketing and strategy. In my head, I'd already sold a thousand franchises of our business, University Window Cleaners. I got in touch with a care home near our university and pitched our business to them. My script went something like this:

'Hello, I'm here with University Window Cleaners and your windows, they're in a real state! I'm surprised the people you have in this care home can see out their windows. Bless them. Let me make you an offer. For whatever price you pay your current window cleaner – who is doing a really bad job –we'll make sure every window in this home is spic and span and we will reduce the price by half.'

Sure enough, we got the contract. When my new business partner came back with the cleaning supplies, we set about cleaning the windows on the bottom floor. We got them gleaming. But then I looked up and realised the building was three or four stories high. We looked at one another, thinking the same thing. How were we going to get up there?

We didn't have a budget for a ladder, so we never got higher than the bottom floor.

It's an apt metaphor for that particular business. Needless to say, we didn't get paid and we weren't hired back.

But it was just another splinter in the arse. There is no failure, only feedback.

Remember that failure is not the opposite of success, it is a part of success.

kush and wizdom.tumblr

We still had the buckets and sponges and other supplies, so we decided to rebrand. We didn't need a ladder to clean cars, so we renamed the business University Car Cleaners. We went house-to-house asking people if they'd like their cars cleaned. We earned what seemed like a fortune. It felt as if we cleaned every single car in Plymouth.

You might be thinking, 'Sure, Toby, it may be easy for you to recover from failure, but I'm not like that.' That's the best part: anyone can learn to train their brain to perceive failure as an opportunity for success.

The idea for this mindset exercise, 'The Disney Model', came from Walt Disney himself, who was known for dreaming bigger than anyone ever dared to dream. We  all know people who are big dreamers, but often they don't get the job done. Walt Disney, as we all know, wasn't one of those people. Practicing this technique will teach you how to be like Walt.

 ## Mindset Exercise: The Disney Model

Spatial positions are important with the Disney model, which uses three different locations. Walt Disney used three different rooms, but you can just use three different chairs.

Chair one: The first chair you sit in is the dreamer chair, and its rules are simple. When you sit in the dreamer chair, you are only allowed to dream. No other activity is allowed in that chair. Your job is to dream – and dream as big as possible, bigger than you have ever dreamed before. Go into a 'Walt Disney' mindset and imagine your business being bigger and more successful than you have ever thought possible. Don't rush. Take your time. Dream big. Allow yourself to get carried away with how big your business could be.

Chair two: Next, move to one of the other chairs. Imagine you are looking in at the dreamer in the dreamer chair. In chair two, you take on the mindset of being a critic. Again, the rules are simple. In chair two, you can only be a critic. The critic looks at the dreamer and comes up with the worst criticism and hardest questions they can think of. They are not allowed to dream. They are not allowed to create. Their role is to be overcritical and to find all the problems and challenges that the dreamer sitting in chair one will meet.

Dissociate from yourself, dissociate from the dreamer – become the critic. Ask questions like, *How are you going to get the financing to do this? How are you going to overcome the objections? Are you really the kind of person who's going to be able to succeed in this? What about those behaviours you have that don't fit with this kind of a business?*

For some people, chair two is going to be far easier than chair one, or vice versa. That's why it's so important to take that different perceptual position and physically move positions to sit in different chairs. Again, don't rush through this chair. Criticise all the negatives and winkle out all the faults. Impose rules and restrictions. Hate the dreamer's dream. This step has a lot to teach you. The critic will give you loads of feedback and you are much better off learning it now before you spend a lot of your time and money on a business that critics will try to tear down in the future.

Chair three: Next, you need someone to offer a real-world perspective. Move to the third chair, so you can see both the dreamer and the critic. In this chair, the rules say you can only be a realist. The realist brings the situation down to a real per-spective or a real model. They look at the critic and attempt to answer their objections from a real-world perspective. This is where you start to see the possibilities before you. You take the feedback you received in chair two and turn it into opportunity to help you achieve a real-world view of the dream you had in chair one.

I completed this exercise when I first thought up the idea of putting waste plastics into roads. The main question I faced in the critic's chair was 'How do I come up with the finances to finance my idea for MacRebur?' When I was in the realist chair, I learned about crowd-funding, and I saw it was a viable option for us. What the realist mindset told me was that I was already using social media, and that a large portion of the population were attracted to my idea of putting waste plastics into roads. As a result of walking through the Disney Model, I decided to ask the crowd to invest in the business. In the end, I gained more than 3,000 investors and £4.2 million of investment into the company in two rounds of funding. It all came about because I sat in the realist's chair, looked in at the dreamer and the critic in their chairs, and attempted to deal with the criticisms to achieve the dream.

After some practice with this exercise, you'll see that you too can train your brain to perceive failure differently. We always have a choice. We can fail and quit (or quit before we even give ourselves the chance to fail), or we can fail, learn what didn't work – and do it differently next time.

Most people fail and give up. I hope that you'll choose to be different.

Chapter Two Principle:

There is no failure, only feedback.

It's All About that Dash

MY WIFE AND I MET AT BOARDING SCHOOL. I WAS A BOARDER, AND SHE WAS a day pupil. I saw an opportunity to get out of the school and go to her place on weekends, and she got a good deal on the sweets from my tuck box. She left and went to a different university from me, but since it took me six years to graduate, we ended up leaving university at exactly the same time.

I've already said that one of my greatest fears on leaving school was having to get a job. It was the same after university. I was happy to jump out of a plane or swim with sharks in Australia, but the thought of getting a job scared the bejesus out of me.

I had a good degree, but I knew I wasn't employable.

(I'm still not, to be honest. If I ever come to you for a job, don't employ me: I'd be awful. I certainly wouldn't want to be the person who employs me.)

I thought, 'What am I going to do? How am I going to fund myself now?' I didn't want to clean cars all my life. I went to see my father, who by that time had retired from the British Forces and – and that's when I came up with my first 'real' business idea.

Suffolk has many bed and breakfasts and hotels, so I asked myself, 'What can I do to build myself a market?' At the time, the internet was a new-fangled thing you could read about in magazines, but people weren't really using it for business (in 1996, there was no social media, not even Google). Still, I thought, 'There's got to be something to this Internet thing'. I spent some time learning HTML coding and used a programme called Dreamweaver to create a website, which I called 'stayinglocal'.

I created a virtual map of the UK split into different regions that visitors clicked. If they clicked on Suffolk, for example, they were sent to another page with a list of bed and breakfasts and hotels. My idea was to sell those businesses the power of the internet, because they were still just using the Yellow Pages. I went to the hotels and said, 'For £70, you can have an advert on my website. Because the web is new, everyone's going to be looking at it, so I think you should advertise here.' My mission was to disrupt old-school marketing techniques and help get B&B's and hotels get onto the 'world wide web'.

Once the business was up and running, I convinced my wife – and her parents – that she shouldn't go on summer holiday with them. She should come to Suffolk, to live with me in my father's house and help run stayinglocal.

We didn't have much ambition beyond supporting ourselves for the summer, but we travelled around the UK, visiting up to ten to twenty bed and breakfasts a day. We parked on one side of the street and went door to door like politicians, only we were selling advertising. By the end of the summer, we had thousands of clients. The business turned over enough to support us over the holidays and gave us a little pocket money to spend on our next projects (though I spent all of mine on beer). At the end of the summer, we decided to end the business and move to London.

Several months later, lastminute.com started up doing exactly what we were doing; it's now a billion-pound business. Another splinter...

Our vision was only to see the business through the summer. In hindsight, we were so shortsighted. Had we set a bigger goal, we could have achieved much greater success.

Today, every entrepreneur hopes to come up with a business idea that becomes a 'unicorn' – a business valued at over $1 billion. It may take years. Most people never find it.

Well, maybe stayinglocal.com was *my* unicorn. I was just too blind to see it. I assumed it was just a cow.

Whatever. At the time, it was OK because we had no greater plans – but I don't make the same mistake now. *Now* I have learned the importance of setting long-term goals. Today, when I start a business, I ask myself, 'Is this a legacy business, or a short-term fix for something?' Short-term fixes are always only that: short-lived and, in the end, pointless.

If you haven't already, I encourage you to go through the Disney Model exercise in Chapter 2 (or do it again!) When you're in Chair 1, the dreamer chair, ask yourself, what will your legacy be?

A legacy is not just a goal for the next year or two (in any case, I think 'goal-setting' is a tired and uninspiring concept).

What I want to know is: What do you stand for? What is your purpose on the planet? What's the purpose of your business?

If you can mix purpose and profit, that's when you've got a great business.

A good friend of mine from university had a passion for cars. After we graduated, he started his own consultancy for Formula One and other motorsports. He had a few people working for him, and he was known nationally as the go-to advisor for his industry. He was a typical English gent, though, who didn't like to talk about his feelings and emotions or even see a doctor.

For as long as I knew him, he suffered from stomach pains. In the end, they got so bad that some of us who cared about him convinced him to see a doctor. He was diagnosed with cancer and told he had three months to live. He died two months later. He was an entrepreneur like me. He was the same age as me. He had kids the same age as my kids. I saw myself in him. When he left, he left without leaving anything for the rest of his family. That broke my heart. He left everything behind – but he didn't leave a legacy.

I decided then that I wasn't going to do the same thing. The businesses I owned at the time were what I called lifestyle businesses: they would fund the life we were leading, without looking towards the future. I looked around at pensions and different ways to invest.

A British entrepreneur I've admired for many years, James Kahn, spoke to me about his 'dash', an idea that comes from a poem by Linda Ellis titled 'The Dash Poem'. The dash is the little line they carve on your headstone between your birth date and your death date.

Since my friend died, I think about the dash very often. What's your dash worth? I'm not only referring to monetary worth, but everything else you're leaving behind. It stands for everything you have from the moment you're born until the moment that you pass away.

Remember: you've only got one dash.

People often build businesses because they want to earn a load of cash, or because they think it's easier than getting a job or for whatever reason. But it really isn't about those things at all. It is all about the dash – the journey from the beginning to the end.

Think about what the future holds for the business you are looking to create. What is it that you can sell or pass on? After you've gone, what will continue to grow from this business you are creating? Don't get stuck on limiting beliefs. Allow yourself to dream big.

 Mindset Exercise: *What if, plus?*

What if, plus is a thought process I've used to create so many businesses.

When I first start out with a new business idea, I ask myself 'What if?' Lots of people do – but so many times they face the challenge of only being able to answer that question about negative scenarios, e.g. *What if it goes wrong? What if it doesn't work? What if I lose all our money?*

So, the advancement of my *What if* question is what I call, *What if, plus.* You have to ask yourself the what if question with a positive mindset. Don't ask, '*What if it doesn't work?*' Ask yourself, '*What if it could work? What if it does work? What if I am the person to do it?*'

Overcome the objections that come to mind and instead ask *What if, plus.* Remember, you aren't just creating a way to make money. You are creating a legacy that can last forever.

- What if I were the one to disrupt this industry?
- What if we were to create this social aspect?
- What if we were able to add this environmental aspect to this business?
- What if this business left something behind for my children and grandchildren?
- What if this business created a better world?

I have asked myself *What if, plus* so often that about five years ago, my wife said, 'Toby, please stop asking yourself that question, because we cannot create any more businesses. We're full up with what we've got.' But, it is a question that is constantly on my mind. And I want it to be on your mind, too.

Chapter Three Principle:

When you are creating a business, you are creating a legacy.

Spot the Gap in the Market

WHEN MY WIFE AND I FIRST MOVED TO LONDON, OUR RENT WAS HORREN-dous. I didn't want to get a job so I decided that, with my degree, I knew enough about science and maths to tutor kids who were struggling through school.

We lived in Hampstead, which has a wealthy Jewish community, so that's who I targeted. I soon realised how big the market potential was. It turned out that a lot of kids struggled with maths and science.

After about six months, my wife quit her job to join me. Together, we formed a business we called 'Capital Tutors'. I don't know if we were first tutoring agency in London, but we were certainly the first to specialise in tutoring the Jewish community.

You have to niche, right?

The business paid our (extortionate) rent. After that, the profit went back into the business. After six years growing the business and the brand (we're both course-and-seminar junkies), we sold Capital Tutors. It still exists today.

Sometimes the golden opportunity is spotting the gap in the market – and it might be right in front of you.

When I look at Sir Richard Branson's businesses – a train line, a mobile service, an airline and more than 400 companies in various fields – they don't focus on creating new things; he makes an industry better by seeing where things aren't working or how they can be improved. That's what progress is about.

Differentiate and Dominate

Quite often, new business owners ask me to name the most powerful marketing strategies I've ever seen. I can say without any hesitation that the most powerful marketing strategy has little to do with advertising, social-media paid marketing, Google SEO, websites or webinars.

Those things won't have any impact unless you uncover and communicate how your business is different from other businesses. Unless you're the inventor of something completely new or the pioneer of a new technique, there's likely to be competitors selling the same services or products as you.

When my partners and I started MacRebur, it was easy to differentiate. The products didn't exist before, and because they were unique, we were quickly able to dominate.

Most businesses, however, have to come up with a way to differentiate.

One way I've mentioned is by disrupting business for good. That's the way of the future. And there are multiple ways you can integrate the concept into your business.

Let's look at some tried and tested ways to claim a unique point of difference:

Product: Can you offer a product that is so unique or fashionable that your business is associated with that offering? Can you extend the product and offer a valuable service to make it more useful to the customer?

Take Tesla, for example. When Elon Musk entered the car market, he wasn't simply selling another car; he was selling *electric* cars. Now he dominates the electric car market and the demand for his cars are high despite being an average of two-and-a-half times more expensive than a traditional car. At the time of writing, the company has not been able to keep up with production, leading to a waiting list of vehicles on backorder. [4]

Service: The same goes for a service. Consulting is usually delivered on an hourly basis, just like coaching, so an effective way to differentiate it is by packaging a consulting engagement based on an outcome, with defined deliverables and a fixed package price. When my wife and I created a coaching programme called '5 Days to Stop Smoking', we didn't charge an hourly rate like the other stop-smoking coaches. Instead, we worked out how many cigarettes each client would smoke over a six-month period and how much that would cost them – it was a lot, because we only worked with heavy smokers – and we charged them what they would usually spend anyway so they didn't feel like they were out of pocket. By month seven, our clients were not only benefiting from being healthier; they also had money in their pockets to spend on other things to enhance their life.

Market niche: If you can carve out a niche or two, you can become the most dominant player serving an industry. This approach has the bonus that you can usually raise your prices dramatically when you specialise in this way.

Offer: Can you become known by the offer you make? In his book *The Irresistible Offer*, Mark Joyner describes an irresistible offer as, 'An *identity-building offer central to a product, service, or company where the believable return on investment is communicated so clearly and efficiently that it's immediately apparent you'd have to be a fool to pass it up.*'

Solve the problem: Can you come up with a solution to something your prospects fear the most? What are the most common fears your prospects have? Focus on communicating how you have the answer to their fears, such as painless dentistry or, the case of Viagra, keeping you 'up'. Uber ran a recruitment campaign with the slogan: 'Get in the driver's seat and make some money'. In other words, your problem is having no money; here's the solution.

Message of value: Businesses often offer services that do not get communicated: extra touches or things you think are implied in the service. I know an office furniture company that offers instant set-up and adopted the message, 'We make your business more valuable'. In other words, you can save time and focus on your business instead of assembling your own furniture. Now, everything the business does is focused on delivering on that statement. Everyone else in the industry simply sells furniture.

Your unique touch: These are small gifts, uniquely yours, like a favour you would do for a friend. My wife and I are fans of Stobo Castle, a spa hotel in Scotland. When we stay overnight and return to our car in the morning, it has always been cleaned inside and out. We rave to our friends and family about this unique touch, and many now stay there as well.

A guarantee: Can you offer a guarantee so strong that no one else in your industry would dream of promising it? This can seem frightening, but you probably guarantee your work anyway – you just don't say so. Come out and boldly announce that you guarantee results and watch what happens.

Customer service: You might know about the legendary over-the-top customer service provided by Nordstrom in the United States. If not, you will know a company that goes the extra mile with their customer service. Create your own over-the-top customer response systems, and word-of-mouth advertising will flow naturally. One of the greatest ways to kick this off is to overdeliver on your first customer contact. Give your customer something more than you promised, like a gift or a related service for free.

Against the competition: You can often create your category niche by looking for holes in the offerings of your competitors. If someone in your industry fails to address a certain problem, solve the problem and use your competition as your point of reference. Looking at our coaching-programme competitors, my wife and I saw a gap in the market and began offering lifetime membership to our courses. This is now one of the main reasons people register for our courses rather than others.

 Mindset Exercise: Believe in the Value You Offer

To discover the value your business offers your customers, try taking the position of a potential client or customer. Step into their shoes and look through their eyes. Then ask yourself two questions:

1. *What is my customer's biggest pain in life?* Visualise, imagine, uncover the pain that people go through with

respect to your product, service or industry. In other words, what is *their* problem? What is keeping them up at night? It is from those pains that your products or services should be designed and marketed: they take the pain away.

2. **What matters to your customer?** Answering this question will elicit some of the values that your customers may have, which will help you determine how to find them, market to them and provide value to their world.

Once you've thought about your customer, move back to your own point of view. Ask yourself, 'How am I the solution to my client's pains?' If you don't know the answer or are unable to come up with a solution, another good exercise is simply to ask five of your ideal clients or customers what their biggest problems are with respect to your product, service or industry.

This will enable you to come up with solutions that remove the pain for your ideal clients. People buy solutions, not products or services.

Chapter Four Principle:

Differentiate and dominate.

The Haters Will Come

AT BOARDING SCHOOL, BULLYING WAS JUST PART OF LIFE.

My gran would occasionally send me treats because I complained about the terrible food we were subjected to at school. She would fill a plastic ice-cream tub with sherbet dips, double dips, refresher bars and rainbow drops and send it to me.

At school the post was all placed in an open box in the staffroom for collection. One of the bullies often got to my parcel before me and stole the contents. I hated him, but he was stronger than me so I didn't fight back. That feeling of injustice still drives me crazy today.

In business, 'injustices' happen every day. If they haven't happened to you yet, hold on. They soon will. No matter how ethical or harmless your business is, the haters will come. They will find you and they will make it their mission to steal your stuff and make you suffer.

In MacRebur, we spend over £200,000 a year on buying 'protection': contracts, insurance, patents, copyrights and trademarks. The haters still come. No matter how big or small your business, they always turn up.

Be prepared.

You can get lawyers to write contracts or apply for patents – but as a friend of mine always says, "A patent will only keep a good man or woman out." I would agree. Most haters aren't good.

Legal actions can only have limited effects. So how can entre-preneurs maintain a good emotional state when the haters arrive?

I've used various strategies over the years but the most effective is one I've called 'FUCM'.

FUCM

You pronounce it as it reads.

In fact, no matter how satisfyingly rude it sounds, FUCM stands for 'Fully Utilise Your Comedy Mindset'. In other words, embrace the laughter!

You have to find a sense of humour in business. If you take everything seriously, you will find yourself overthinking and getting stressed about even tiny challenges. Run your business through trial and error, dare to 'give things a go' and use a comedy mind-set to deal with everyday challenges – and the haters won't be able to hurt you.

There's no need to build yourself up as a serious business person who cringes at a slight mistake or gets offended easily by feedback from the haters – or even from your customers.

In some ways everyone is a dickhead, just some people get away with it easier than others. Expect to make thousands of mistakes in your business and expect the haters to point out how much of a dickhead you actually are. Then think to yourself 'FUCM'.

Laugh it off. Your comedy mindset is the essence of living a satis-fying, productive, fulfilling and fun life. The more you cultivate your comedy mindset, the more you learn and the more you'll achieve – and the better your business will be.

Most people are damaged individuals in some way but if we can give ourselves enough laughs, we can keep our inner demons at bay.

The familiar adage 'laughter is the best medicine' comes from the fact that humour reduces stress levels and improves mental health.

> **Mindset Exercise: FUCM**
>
> 1. Think of the last time someone hurt you or discredited your ideas. Picture them and repeat after me 'FUCM, FUCM, FUCM'.
> 2. Now find three things you can laugh about when you think of that same situation.
> 3. Embrace your comedy mindset and the haters won't be able to touch you.

Dealing with Anxiety and Overwhelm — 'Purple Liquid' Meditation

Another effective strategy I recommend to maintain a solid emotional state is the following:

I used to experience 'overwhelm' a lot, especially when I first started in business. I got so many Vitamin B injections from a doctor friend that I became dependent on them for a few years. Whether the vitamins actually made me feel better or it was a placebo, I didn't care: I wanted to get out from overwhelm, and it worked. But I didn't want to rely on an injection to help me feel better and I felt I wanted to take control of my emotions myself.

As a hypnotherapist and coach, my wife had learned a technique from a 'stop-smoking' practitioner, Valerie Austin, who had written a script my wife gave me to try. Adapting Valerie's script, I came up with my own short meditation I've called 'purple liquid'. It has the same effect as the Vitamin B injections.

If you suffer from overwhelm and anxiety, I recommend visiting my website where I have recorded an audio file. Get yourself comfortable and then listen to me while I talk you through my technique: www.tobymccartney.com/businessReLOVEution

Mindset Training

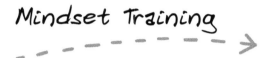

My father-in-law worked for the health council as a trainer and had just been on a course in Neuro-Linguistic Programming (NLP), an approach to communication and personal development based on the neural processing of the brain. He raved about the course and urged Kate and I to pack our bags for Orlando, Florida, to try it for ourselves (courses weren't readily available in the UK).

The course changed our lives. I felt as if someone had painted another colour in the rainbow for me. NLP gave a scientific explanation of all the stuff I understood intuitively, like keeping a comedy mindset, and why it worked.

We came home inspired to bring NLP home with us. After all, we needed to earn back what we'd just paid for the course. We had qualified as NLP Practitioners, so we could share our newfound tools with others who could benefit from what we had learnt. We'd absorbed our trainer's message to 'Believe in yourself and make it happen' – so, rather than just becoming coaches or practitioners, we started the British Board of Neuro-Linguistic Programming. We made it happen.

We converted the box room in our London flat into an office, from which we created the BBNLP membership organisation, designed to offer support to other practitioners in the field. We produced our own websites and logos, along with a full-colour magazine, *The*

Model Magazine, that eventually had a circulation of 11,000 people worldwide.

The NLP industry wasn't always welcoming. The haters soon turned up, because we were the new kids on the block, young and without experience. But we were on a mission to disrupt the NLP industry for good by creating the BBNLP membership organisation.

I was hounded online by a man who called himself the 'NLP police', who was basically a cyber bully. He created a fictitious website called 'Bored with NLP' with images of mine and my wife's heads pasted onto porn scenes – Kate was quite offended, but to be honest I quite enjoyed the pictures. It was hideously stressful at the time, but key NLP trainers and people within the industry went out of their way to support us.

Not everyone is going to support you disrupting their market. A bigshot in the NLP community summoned us to his office south of London one day to find out who we thought we were to set up the BBNLP.

It was not a meeting of minds. He was 50 years old and we were 22 years young. Like the industry itself, he was set in his ways, while we had nothing to lose. He was very skeptical, critical and generally negative. He didn't like us one bit. Kate and I had to scrape ourselves off the ground. We thought to ourselves, 'We either have to pack this in now or go full steam ahead'.

After sleeping on it that night we thought 'FUCM'! We did it anyway!

About six months later, I checked my email and said to Kate, 'You're not going to believe who just signed up to become a corporate member with us.' It was the same man who had dressed us down. It was such a significant moment. To be honest, I've wondered whether that was his intention all along, to test us in such a way that would propel our motivation. If we get to choose our beliefs, maybe it's nice to think that one of the leaders of our industry looked at us and thought, 'You know what? I'm going to play the long game. I'm going to wind them up, but if they can make this work, I'll join them later.'

In hindsight, we prefer to believe that he had our best intentions at heart.

I look back now to how young, naïve and enthusiastic I was then, and how badly I was treated, and I realise that that experience in my early twenties contributed to the very thick skin I have today. There aren't many days now where I don't use the FUCM technique.

Many years later, we knew MacRebur would upset some people. We were there to disrupt the oil, asphalt and plastics industries, which include some powerful players. We had a barrage of critics telling us we were the worst people on the face of the planet. We had to accept the fact that not everybody was going to like us.

When we started the business, I was invited to a council meeting. I felt very pleased with myself. *A local authority has invited me in*, I thought. Then I received an email saying, 'Bring some cash because you guys are paying for the lunch'.

They were literally just after a free lunch. At a meeting to which *they'd* invited *us*.

The amount of criticism I received for MacRebur might astonish other CEOs. *Nobody* thought plastic roads were a good idea when we started; nobody had anything good to say about the idea.

Get used to being treated badly in business. Especially if your business is built to disrupt. Haters are going to hate, but don't let them stop you from doing whatever it is you want to do. Sometimes you might just need to buy them a beer and build some rapport, and if that doesn't work, FUCM.

Mindset Exercise: Feedback from the Future

Sir Richard Branson (known as "Dr. Yes") uses a technique where he imagines what his future self might offer as advice today and writes himself a letter. What would you say to yourself from five years into the future? What would your future-self advise you to do now?

Here is some of Sir Richard's advice from the letters he wrote to himself:

"You've never gone into business to make money, but instead always wanted to make a positive difference in people's lives."

"The sky is no longer the limit and the future will be so bright, if you continue to look for opportunities where others see challenges."

"Keep having fun, taking risks and looking for the best in people."

"Keep looking at the world with wide-eyed enthusiasm, and believing that together we are more powerful than the problems that confront us."

"Continue to take chances. In the future how 'lucky' you are in business will be determined by how willing you are to take calculated risks."

"Your ability to take calculated risks and your incurable optimism will lead to great heights – both in business and in life."

Chapter Five Principle:

Don't let the naysayers deter you.

The Secret to Singular Successes

I HAD BEEN PROMISING MY FOUR YEAR-OLD DAUGHTER THAT I WOULD FIX HER Peppa Pig doll for weeks, but when I found her crying in her bedroom with the two parts of Peppa in her hands, it was time to live up to my promise.

The only place still open that Sunday evening was Mrs. Shields Ironmongers in the small town near our home. I arrived just before closing time and asked for some superglue.

'What is the glue for?' Mrs. Shields asked politely.

I explained in great detail how I really needed to fix Peppa Pig that night otherwise I would feel like I was letting my daughter down… As I started pouring out my whole life story, Mrs. Shields interrupted me. 'Plastic then?' she asked.

'Umm, yes,' I responded as if I had just been caught doing something wrong by my headmistress. 'Peppa is plastic.'

'Well,' Mrs. Shields said, 'I don't think any of the brands I have will do the trick. They tend to fix the problem for a short time, but then the plastic breaks again and you are back where you started. What can you expect for £2.00?'

'True, I guess....' I muttered and turned to leave.

'However...' her voice came from behind me, 'I do have another type of glue that I don't normally sell to just anyone...' She fumbled around in a draw before pulling out a tatty old box marked 'Impact – high strength, instant bond adhesive'. 'This is what I use and it really works. You might not want to pay the price though. It's £6.99!'

'I'll take it...' I said quickly, and left the shop feeling delighted with my purchase.

Mrs. Shields was right. The stuff that's usually not available to 'just anyone', the stuff that's kept under the counter, the stuff that's really sticky; that stuff really does work. Peppa was fixed and I was a hero daddy – all thanks to Mrs. Shields.

I recommend you take a leaf out of her book. Find one thing you can be good at or have knowledge in that others in your team or network do not. That one thing that will stick in people's minds that relates to you. Learn about, and become skilled in, a particular aspect of your business. Become the Vlogging expert, or learn about webinars; be the social media go-to, or learn about PR or a particular marketing technique that you can do well and get results.

Not only will this skill mean you will become known as an expert. It will also help you build confidence in yourself, knowing that you can do something others can't. During the school holidays I loved to visit my grandparents in Morecambe, where my Grandfather would take me to play pool at the Pleasure Land arcade. I got pretty handy on the pool table and started to play for the local team. When I got to senior school, I wasn't academic, I wasn't the best at football or the fastest runner – but I was good at pool. It began to define me and I became known as the best pool player in the school. There wasn't a school badge for it, but I wore the title with pride. Being the best at something helped me build confidence in myself that translated into other parts of my life. It didn't matter that I wasn't the best at anything else – I had my one thing I could do well.

To this day, I find one thing I can do that others don't or can't do. For example, I'm a pretty awful singer, but I've learned one song that I can sing pretty well if I'm ever forced into Karaoke and won't embarrass myself. I've learned one tune I can play on the guitar, just in case anyone ever asks, 'Do you play an instrument?' I've learned enough Turkish phrases so that if someone asks 'Do you speak another language?' I can confidently say 'I know enough Turkish to get by', which few other people can (apart from the Turkish, of course). I learnt the rules to American football, even though I have never played the sport, so I have some knowledge when I'm socialising with American clients.

I like to find one thing I can be good at or know about, that I suspect people will be surprised by when they ask 'Do you?' or 'Can you?'

Building a Confidence Muscle

There's no good feeling in looking bad, and often our fears can sabotage us and hold us back.

Starting something new can be daunting and can seem like a whole load of extra effort. We've all been there. It's easy to say 'no' to new things out of fear of looking bad, but you will never fulfil your full potential if you don't try new things.

If you get really good at one thing, you will never look bad at doing it. Even if you are faced with someone asking you to do something you don't think you can, you can always rely on the things you already can do. Try saying, 'I'm not sure about X, but I can help by doing Y'.

It might start with a small thing you can get good at, something others don't currently do, but in no time at all you will find that you are wanting to learn new things. Building confidence in yourself is like building a muscle at the gym. If you do the workouts, it will grow. And like exercise, building confidence in yourself can become addictive.

Mindset Exercise: Stacking Anchors

I use this brilliant technique to help build a 'confidence muscle'. It can be used to help you build any positive emotion you need.

In NLP, 'anchoring' is the term used for the process by which you capture the peak of a positive emotion. The *anchored* state can then be recalled or reactivated through a gesture, picture, touch or sound. In the words of NLP co-creator Richard Bandler, 'Anchoring refers to the tendency for any one element of an experience to bring back the entire experience.'

In 1902, Dr. Edwin B. Twitmyer submitted a paper to the American Medical Association called 'Stimulus Response'. It outlined the hammer-to-knee reflex. The American Medical Association was not interested. In 1904, the Russian Ivan P. Pavlov read Twitmyer's paper. In 1936, after years of research with dogs, he submitted a paper to the Russian Medical Society called 'Conditioned Reflexes', and got the credit for discovering stimulus-response. He anchored the sound of a tuning fork to when the dogs felt hungry; eventually, the mere sound of the tuning fork made the dogs salivate.

Anchoring is fundamentally the process of stimulus-response. There are many kinds of anchors.

Many behavioural psychologists believe we operate our lives totally with conditioned reflexes. Many also believe that learning is setting up new anchors and responding to them.

Under certain circumstances an anchor will last forever, particularly if an experience was highly emotionally charged. The key is to be able to anchor a state in any person at any time in any modality.

And here's how you do it. Remember the acronym RACER...

Recall: Recall a past positive vivid experience. The best states to anchor are those that occur naturally and that are vivid and highly associated states. Can you remember a time when you were totally relaxed (or happy or confident, or so on)? Can you remember a specific time? Many people remember a number of experiences. Remember one specific time.

Associate: Imagine being in that same positive experience, looking through your own eyes now. Associate into what you can see, hear and feel. Allow those positive feelings to overwhelm you.

Change state: As you reach the peak of that positive state, offer yourself a word, or phrase, or gesture that you can use again to remind you of what it's like to experience this emotion. Sometimes a clenched fist works. This becomes your trigger to fire whenever you want to be reminded of this emotion.

Exit: As the positive state starts to drop away (after about 10 to 30 seconds), re-associate into the now. It's important to experience the non-state and move in and out of the emotion to build the muscle. You can test the power of your emotion by simply reminding yourself of the gesture, phrase or word trigger that you gave yourself above.

Repeat: Repeat the process above until you have enough of the positive emotion. It's like going to the gym, you need to go a number of times before you start to see any results. Test your anchor again until you are satisfied you have enough of the positive emotion associated.

Chapter Six Principle:

Find one thing you are good at and become known for it.

CHAPTER SEVEN

Be Your Own Guru

IN CASE YOU HAVEN'T BEEN ABLE TO TELL, MY FASCINATION WITH SIR RICHARD Branson didn't end with my nine-year-old self. Later in life, I read his books and vowed that I would meet him someday.

One year, Kate and I were on our usual holiday in Puerto Pollensa, Majorca. On the last night of our holiday, we sat outside a restaurant in the town square on a beautiful evening.

It was 2007, the start of the recession, and Branson was trying to do a deal with the bank Northern Rock. Perhaps things weren't going well, because he obviously decided to go away for the week-end – to Puerto Pollensa. He walked past where we were sitting. I said to Kate, 'Oh, my god. That's Richard Branson. That's my guru. He just walked past. He's a real person!'

I was so excited a little bit of wee came out.

Half an hour later, Sir Richard and his entourage of people came back and sat down two tables away.

A lot of wee came out at that point.

I couldn't contain myself. 'Oh, my god. Look over my shoulder, he's just over there.' Kate said, 'God, that's really him. It's not a lookalike. It is really him.'

Then she said, 'Go and speak to him.' I refused. It was surely a step too far.

I had all these thoughts in my head *What do I even call him? Is Sir Richard too sucky-up? And Dicky isn't sucky up enough, right? I think I'd call him Mr. Branson.* But it was all irrelevant because I wasn't going to speak to him.

Until Kate got involved. 'Listen, Toby', she said. 'You teach people every day to have faith in themselves and the courage to take every opportunity that comes their way. You've got to go and speak to him.'

I said, 'I know I teach it, but I'm not doing it.'

And that was the end of it, I thought. But Kate had different ideas. Which is why a few minutes later, I stood up from out table, put my hands behind my back and looked down at the floor—like a school-boy— and walked over to his table. Talking at what seemed like a thousand miles an hour I said, 'Mr. Branson, I really love you. I like girls and everything, but I really love you. You're absolutely amazing. I wrote to you when I was nine, and you wrote back. I've read all your books. I've watched everything about you. I just think you're an amazing person.'

It felt like I went on forever, but it must have been about 30 seconds. And do you know what happened? He looked up at me and said, 'Pull up a chair.'

I've never sat down faster in my life. We spoke for two and a half hours. His meal went cold. His wife was noticeably irritated. His son, Sam, and daughter, Holly, lost interest and started wandering around. At last I thought, I've outstayed my welcome. So, I said, 'Thank you, Mr. Branson, it's been wonderful to meet you. And thank you all for your time.'

I walked back with my confident Essex-boy, big-balls walk, to the table where poor Kate had been left on her own for two and a half hours. She could have been mad but she was thrilled. 'What did he say? What did you talk about? What did he say?' she asked. I answered casually, 'Oh, we just talked about business, you know how it is.'

I was so cocky. But in the end, what I told her was that I didn't get the business tools and tips I might have expected. Instead, what I got from the experience was simply that Sir Richard is just a bloke. I know that's not really inspiring. It's not high-fiving the arrival of a salad like Americans do. But it's what stood out to me: he's just a bloke, doing what he loves.

In that moment, I learned all I needed to learn from Sir Richard. I just need to be who I am and do the stuff that I love, not stuff I'm made to do or that I'm forcing myself to do. And I realised that no-one else needs to be my guru. I am my own guru. I have all the resources I need to achieve the things I want to achieve if I do the things I love to do and I'm myself while I'm doing them.

You may need some help making the mental shift from someone who looks up to someone else to being the person you look up to. Here's an exercise to help you shift perspectives.

 Mindset Exercise: Perceptual Positions

1. Identify a limiting belief you want to address. For example, a belief that *I'm not good enough to go into business*. Think about what pictures, sounds and feelings are present for you when you think this.
2. When you think about that belief, visualise sitting in a different seat and looking back at yourself, as your guru.
3. Imagine becoming the person you most admire on the planet. Imagine what it's like to be him or her. Consider an obstacle you have now—such as a limiting belief—and ask yourself, *What would (your guru) do?* Or, *What would (your guru) say?* This is an actual process where you become your guru in your mind.

4. Look back at yourself, sitting in the other seat, and advise yourself from the position of the guru. What is it that the person you see sitting in the chair should believe that is different from that old limiting belief? How could he or she make this change now?

Imagine what resources this guru has that you need to have in order to get rid of your limiting belief. Then imagine beaming those resources into yourself, so that you can have them as well. This exercise actually causes those resources to flow through you, through your neurology. How could you not be the change that you have found within yourself?

You are starting to experience the change right now just by thinking about it!

Be your own guru and call upon your guru with this technique whenever you need him/her.

Balls to the Wall

KATE AND I ONCE ATTENDED A TRAINING PROGRAMME RUN BY JOHN GRINDER, one of the original co-creators of NLP. He had heard about our magazine, so he agreed to our pie-in-the-sky invitation to lunch.

Just as Kate had forced me to approach Sir Richard Branson in Majorca, I knew I had to build up enough courage to invite John Grinder to become an organisational member or sponsor of our organisation, the BBNLP. Getting him on board meant many of his followers would also join. If it was good enough for the co-founder of NLP to join, surely they'd figure it was good enough for everyone.

Let me give you a piece of advice, gratis. Driving the creator of your whole field of business—your Einstein, your Henry Ford, your Steve Jobs—to lunch, in *your* car, is nerve-wracking. Terrifying. I've never been more frightened of having an accident. I was sure John was analysing my driving skills, or lack of them, as well as everything else: he used to work for the CIA, so I knew he could read body language.

At lunch we ordered clams in a shell that had to be eaten with our hands. A bad choice for a business lunch. Eating demanded virtually all of our attention, but we eventually found the courage to make a pitch to him. We told him we knew we were the new kids on the block, but did he want to be on our board of neuro-linguistic programming experts? It was a big ask and looked certain to end in cringe-worthy embarrassment. But after we sincerely pitched our concept and vision, he looked at us both and smiled: 'You know, I think you might just be naïve enough to pull this off.'

We were chuffed, of course, but also a little dumbfounded. Kate and I turned to each other afterward and said, 'I think that was a yes'. We excitedly told everybody that John Grinder, a guy no-one else had gotten access to, was now on our board. In reality, of course, all he'd said was, 'You might just be naïve enough to make this work'.

And I *was*. We were both naïve enough to make it work. And eventually John did end up joining as an organisational member.

The lesson here: If you're going to go 'out', go balls-to-the-wall out.

Badass Brews

I'll tell you what I mean. A few years ago, I met James Watt, or 'Brewdog James' as he is sometimes known. James is CEO & cofounder of BrewDog, which produces various types of ales and lagers.

The business was founded in Fraserburgh, a small town in Aberdeenshire, Scotland, in April 2007 and today is worth over £2 billion.

James and his business partner, Martin, only know how to go balls-to-the-wall out, and their story inspires many modern entrepreneurs who, like James, want to disrupt business for good. James and Martin started BrewDog precisely because they were bored of the industrially brewed lagers and stuffy ales that dominated the UK beer market.

At twenty-four years old, they leased a building in Fraserburgh, took out some bank loans, bought brewing equipment and started making tiny batches of hardcore craft beers. At the time, they filled all the bottles by hand and sold them at local markets or out of the back of a van.

In 2011, James and Martin raised over £2.2 million through crowdfunding, welcoming more than 5,000 new shareholders in the company. By 2015, they announced plans to hire an additional 130 employee and opened 17 new bars in cities such as Aberdeen and Glasgow.

To mark the company's tenth anniversary, James and Martin made a commitment to change the way they do business. They pledged to give away 20% of their profits every year: 10% would go to their staff and 10% to charity. In 2018, they broke the world record for Equity crowdfunding, closing at over £126 million. And they launched the BrewDog Blueprint: a manifesto for the future, including their commitment to disrupting business for good.

Sometimes, I meet people in business and can't help but think *I want to be just like them.* James Watt is one of those people. I love his no-messing-around, balls-to-the-wall attitude!

You Can't Eat a Mars Bar and Still Lose Weight

Along with our coaching business, Kate and I run mastermind groups for entrepreneurs. The intention of the groups is to give members opportunities to help each other solve problems and develop themselves. The core value of any good mastermind group is the synergy of energy, motivation and commitment, as well as the willingness to learn and grow together.

One of our coaching clients was on a journey to lose weight. She tried every diet, was faced with many challenges and struggled with her own mindset. But then she managed to get it sorted. She learned some new skills and put them together into a programme for people struggling to lose weight or who are not as fit as they wish to be. Shortly after she joined one of our masterminding groups, she sent me a message saying that she was dropping out because she didn't feel as if she was good enough to be in business for herself.

Feedback like that is so frustrating to receive—especially because I know she *is* good enough to be in business for herself. If she were to play full out, she would see the results. I walked her through an exercise to work on eliminate her limiting beliefs and build up empowering beliefs instead (the exercise is at the end of the chapter).

As entrepreneurs, it is crucial to rid ourselves of those beliefs that hold us back. I believe that every modern entrepreneur has to live by four rules:

1. Be prepared for turbulent times. You can't let the conditions determine your success.
2. 'Nil Sine Laboure' – this was my old school Latin motto and means 'Nothing without hard work'. Modern entrepreneurs must be prepared for hard work and be disciplined in consistently taking action.
3. Have a high level of creativity. Be creative in your approach to solving the challenges that come your way. Creativity is key to most entrepreneurial successes.
4. Play all-out. Take massive action every time!

In my client's weight-loss programme, she would talk about how her clients would not give it a full go: they would follow the programme, but then have a Mars Bar for lunch. If someone wants to lose weight, they have to play full out; they can't keep eating pies and not exercising, or they're not going to lose weight. It's almost as simple as that.

My client had managed to sort that out with her weight loss, but she hadn't yet transferred those skills into her business life.

As an entrepreneur, you've got to be all in. A business is like a love affair. You've got to be as passionate about your business as you are about your partner. You've got to be willing to wake up with it in the morning and go to bed with it at night. If you're not thinking about it all the time, then you're not all in.

I've always been able to take action in the moment and often can't wait to get cracking on with tasks: I hate putting things off until later. Procrastination is an enemy of business, and taking massive action fast is key to most entrepreneurial success. Although it sounds counterintuitive, I often use meditation as a cue to get me ready to take massive action if I find I'm slipping into a CBA—'Can't Be Arsed'—mindset. I use the Bellows Breath meditation exercise on page 125 two or three times a week to pick up my energy levels and remotivate myself to get things done.

Beliefs Are a Choice

I used to enjoy watching the comedian Dom Jolly in *Trigger Happy TV*, a hidden-camera comedy show. In one particular sketch he wore a doctor's white coat and stood on the pavement directing people off the kerb, where he had drawn a chalk outline of a body, onto a busy road full of traffic. Everyone did as he instructed them. There were no police, no yellow tape, just an obviously hand-drawn chalk outline on the ground and Dom Jolly directing people to step out onto the road and into danger. Why didn't they simply walk through the obvious trick he was playing on them? It made no sense—and yet the answer is simple. He was wearing a doctor's white coat, and in the back of everyone's mind that coat is such strong evidence of credibility and conviction that it defies what the logical mind clearly knows is a joke.

Our beliefs originate from what we see, hear and feel—and the more we see, hear and feel them, the more we believe them. The sources of our limiting beliefs include the environment around us (like a white coat), events and behaviours, our skills, capabilities

75

and knowledge, past experiences, our values, who we believe we are and what our purpose becomes. One of the biggest misconceptions people often harbour is that belief is a static, intellectual concept. Nothing could be further from the truth!

Beliefs are a choice. We have the power to choose our beliefs and we can change them. Because our beliefs become our reality, it's vital that we choose to believe in ourselves and our abilities.

 Mindset Exercise: The Belief Unblocker

Here is a simple exercise to help you eliminate any limiting beliefs that may hold you back, while simultaneously building up empowering beliefs that will serve you better.

Choose to work on a belief that has held you back in the past and that keeps challenging you and stopping you from achieving success.

1. Identify where the belief comes from. How long have you had it? When did you decide to have that belief?

2. Now identify some specifics around the belief:
   - What is important for that belief to play out in regards to the environment?
   - What behaviours underpin that limiting belief?
   - What skills, capabilities and knowledge are required to have that belief?
   - What past experiences led to that belief?
   - What is important to you about having that belief?
   - With that belief playing out, who are you and how does that belief affect your purpose?

3. Now imagine stepping out of your body and becoming your guru – whatever all-knowing, solution-focused being you might imagine. Become him or her (or it!). Now, as

your guru, try going back to the time and place when you decided to have that limiting belief. This may take some time to achieve.

4. Offer your guru's solutions to yourself about what choices you could make now to decide to believe something different:

- What's important to you, as the guru, about this new empowering belief?
- What different choices would you make to change the environment to fit in with this new belief, and how does that in turn affect your behaviours?
- What skills, capabilities and knowledge do you, as the guru, carry with you to harness your new belief now? With this new belief in place, who are you?
- What is your true purpose and how can you fulfil this purpose now with this new belief in place?

Notice how you realign to fit in with this new empowering belief. When you feel that the new empowering belief is in place, move back into your own body and realise that you are in fact your own guru. You have personal empowerment. You can choose to believe in whatever serves you – and you can eliminate any unwanted beliefs at any time you wish with these simple thoughts.

Chapter Eight Principle:

If you're going to play the game, play full out.

I Don't Believe in Charity

In 2005, MY WIFE, KATE AND I WENT TO INDIA TO RUN A TRAINING PRO-gramme. Rather egotistically, I had visions of myself helping the people in India ('Don't worry: Toby's here!'). In fact, I learned far more in India than I taught anyone – so much that we named our eldest daughter India in honour of our amazing experiences in the country.

In Kerala, Kate and I visited an orphanage for children whose parents had either passed away or abandoned them. We met the director of the charity to work out how he almost single-handedly took care of 200 children! Kate and I also fell in love with a little girl named Sughandy, which means 'sweet smelling'. She kept coming over towards us, full of curiosity, peeking at us from behind the corner. We said to the director, 'Tell us all about this little girl. Can we sponsor her? We want to help.'

Back at home, we decided to donate 20% of our profit to the orphanage to help Sugandhi and the others. But what we realised after a few months was that we were essentially using the donation as a marketing tool. We would say to our customers, 'We take this money and give it to these poor orphan children in India'. We genuinely wanted to help the children, of course, but we felt very uneasy that we seemed to be benefiting from our gesture. It didn't feel like the right thing to do.

In any case, to be honest, the money we were giving them didn't allow them to do much other than build a new toilet block or put a new roof on a building. It wasn't really making a difference to the children's lives. Rather than just give money away, I wanted to work in a much more entrepreneurial way. I wanted to create something that was world changing – or that would at least change the world of the children in the orphanage.

Then, at a conference, I met an American guy who came in with these weird shoes with separate toes. I asked, 'What the hell have you got on your feet?' And he said, 'Vibram FiveFingers. They're a running shoe that get runners back to the idea of barefoot running. They're much better for your body than shoes that are built up at the back.'

At the time I was training to run the London Marathon, so I was intrigued. At home, I tried to buy some shoes but I couldn't find them anywhere. In the end, I phoned Vibram and asked, 'Where can I buy your shoes?' They said, 'They're not available in the UK yet, they're only in the States.' At first I thought, *Well, I guess I'm not going to get a pair*. But then I said to them, 'What if I sell your shoes in the UK? I think there's a real market for them so I'd like UK distribution rights. But here's the deal: I don't want to make any profit.'

They must have thought I was crazy.

Maybe, but my madness had reason to it. I'd worked out that, for every five pairs of shoes that I was able to sell online, I'd make £200 profit. I would take that profit to India and use it to help single women in poverty start businesses, from seam-stressing to candle making to basket weaving. I would teach the women a money system I'd learned from my Gran, which I called the 'jam jar system'. my Gran would take her old-age pension and put 10% into each of various jam jars: one for the gas bill, one for the electric bill, one for groceries and so on.

My idea was that, once these women's businesses turned a profit, they would put 10% of that profit into each jam jar for their bills – but another 10% into a jar that would go towards adopting children who couldn't get into the orphanage in Kerala. Although the orphanage could sleep 200 children, there were another 200 children on a waiting list.

Orphans in India have no opportunities. They are in the lowest caste, so they can't marry outside of it or get a job outside it: they're stuck for life. But when these women adopted them, the children were no longer orphans: they became members of a business family, giving them the opportunity for a better life.

As we sold Vibram shoes online, the money went straight to the outreach project to set up businesses for people in poverty. Once those businesses are in profit, the women can adopt up to three children.

By selling shoes through our website, Toby's Shoes, we helped more than 500 families out of poverty. The scheme continues, although now it is part of the outreach programmes we set up across the globe. We continue to sponsor children every month. Some of the children in the orphanage have gone on to become nurses or doctors and get all sorts of jobs.

Women in the programme have been highly enthusiastic about adopting children. A blind widow adopted two orphans, who look after her, and she also learned how to sew and became a professional seamstress (as part of the programme, old wind-up or treadle Singer sewing machines were donated from Lockerbie, where Mac-Rebur is based, and sent to India.) With the money she has raised through her new sewing business, the widow built a home, hiring builders to construct it so that she can feel her way around, so she always knows where she is. It's been a hugely successful endeavour, and it has effected far more long-term change than just funding an orphanage through a charity.

Building Entrepreneurs

I've thought a lot about charity.

In places in India like Mumbai or Bangalore, where you get stuck in traffic, children knock on the car window and put their hands out, begging. There is so much poverty.

I used to always give the kids money. Then one day when I was in the car with an Indian friend, Arul, a little boy knocked on the window and put his hand out. I wound down the window to give him some money but Arul stopped me and said, 'Do not give him any money unless it's a trade because otherwise you're just giving charity.' If I could create an education or exchange behind that money, it wouldn't be charity, and I'd be able to help them retain some dignity – almost like the beginning of a business. Arul told me, 'What we do to encourage people is to tell them, "Go and get me something to sell to me – anything you can find…" It could be cotton buds to clean ears, or plastic cups or anything else that could be traded in exchange for money.'

The children have to find somewhere to source and then sell those products; effectively putting them in business for themselves rather than just begging. Giving money is only going to perpetuate the problem: there's always going to be a need for begging. Whereas if the beggar gives you those cotton buds in return for some of your money, then it's effectively a trade and there's education along with the transaction. It's not charity.

If I give money to charity, I never really know where it goes. If I create a social scheme as with Toby's Shoes, however, it's not about just giving that money to make me feel better and merely hoping that it's doing some good. I'm having a direct and observable impact on individuals and a social system.

I don't believe in charity, but I do believe in mixing purpose and profit in disrupting business for good. Instead of being a settler and taking the easy route of charity, find a way to be a pioneer.

Modern Pioneers

Disrupting business for good comes in many different forms. I've been inspired by Warby Parker, an American online retailer of pre-scription glasses and sunglasses. Warby Parker started out by solving a problem: eyewear is too expensive. They cut out the middle-man and offer trendy glasses at a fraction of the price directly to their customers. Warby Parker uses a home try-on offer, where they send customers five different frames of their choice to try on before they make the decision to purchase.

The company also addressed the lack of access to corrective glasses for nearly one billion people worldwide: 15% of the world's population.[5] Knowing that a functional pair of glasses can be life-changing, Warby Parker created their programme Buy a Pair, Give a Pair. They make a monthly donation to nonprofit partners such as Vision Springs, which brings prescription eyewear to people in developing countries. Warby Parker have distributed more than 4 million pairs of glasses since the programme began in 2010.

Ben & Jerry's, meanwhile, made headlines in summer 2020 for their corporate activism,[6] when they loudly supported the Black Lives Matter Movement.[7] They have a long history of corporate social responsibility, such as through their Caring Dairy programme, which offers their dairy farmers a programme to evaluate, imple-ment and continuously improve sustainable agriculture practices. The company supports small family farms through the Ben and Jer-ry's Foundation and they encourage the employees to give back to their communities, in addition to offering grants for social justice programmes.

There are many examples of positive change out there. Just ask yourself the broad question: how can I be a pioneer and make socially responsible business decisions that mix purpose with profit?

Chapter Nine Principle:

Pioneer your way to purpose and profit.

There is Money in Old Muck

THE IDEA FOR THE BUSINESS, MACREBUR, BEGAN AT MY SIX-YEAR-OLD daughter's school assembly. Parents were invited to sit and listen to what the children had been finding out about.

That particular week was based around the oceans. The teacher asked all the children, 'So, what lives in our oceans?' One little girl put her hand up and said, 'Fish.' A little boy said, 'Whales and dolphins.' And then my little girl put her hand up and said, 'Plastics. Plastics live in our oceans.'

I'll always remember the teacher's reaction. She took a step back and I worried, for a moment, that she thought my daughter had done the wrong project. In fact, my little girl had done a little bit of research on Google, using voice search. She'd worked out that, by the time she reached my age, there would be more plastics in our oceans than fish.

When she told me the story, I'd had a dad moment. I thought, 'I don't want my little girl growing up in a world where there'll be more plastics in our oceans than fish.'

I believe the state of the oceans is my generation's fault, and our challenge to overcome. I wanted to do something about it, but I didn't really know what yet.

At the same time, my mother-in-law came to visit from her home three miles away and announced, 'Because of the poor quality of the roads between our house and your house, I'm not going to come and visit you anymore.'

I thought that was marvellous to be honest. But my wife thought otherwise, and told me I had to do something about the roads.

Yeah, right. I'm not a mechanic. I don't know how to fix a car, and I certainly didn't know how to fix roads. Or so I thought. Then I remembered something I'd seen in India, where people were being employed as 'pickers'. A picker's job is to go to landfill sites and pick out by hand anything that might be recyclable. They were taking things made out of thick and durable plastic, such as Ribena and juice cartons, cutting them up then turning them into purses and wallets. Waterproof!

Even more genius, these kids were setting up next to the leather shops where tourists would go to buy expensive wallets, belts and so on. So rather than buying leather, tourists started buying the wallets made from recycled plastic. They were cheaper and more environmentally friendly – but they also had a story behind them. Remember I said in Chapter One that businesses of the future need to have either an environmental or a social impact? These kids had figured out how to do both. They took something that would otherwise go in the landfill and created a desirable product, while simultaneously supporting their families.

That was their story. It's an important part of creating any environmental or social business. You have to create a narrative, because it's that narrative that people buy into.

I was absolutely inspired by what the children in India were able to recycle. What they couldn't recycle, such as plastic rubbish, they put into potholes.

India's pothole problem is even worse than ours – though not by much! They drive about on Tuk Tuks, mopeds and bicycles that are lethal if they hit a pothole. So the kids filled the potholes with plastic, poured diesel on top and then lit it, so the plastic melted to fill and seal in the hole.

I thought, 'That's a solution. That's what I'm going to do.'

I gathered all our home-waste plastics and filled all the potholes between my mother-in-law's house and ours. I shredded the plastics, filled the holes, poured on the diesel, lit it and melted the plastic down.

I got into a lot of trouble with the police. It turns out the local authority and the police force frowned upon trying to set light to the road.

I should have stopped the first time I was told off. But to be honest, I was less scared about going to prison than about going to my mother-in-law and telling her I couldn't mend the potholes. Anyway, I figured that if I got in trouble again, it was more likely to force the local authority into filling the potholes themselves.

Most of all, I believed that I was doing the right thing. Bending the rules to create good is how change comes; that is how we disrupt. Rules sometimes keep us from being innovative.

I couldn't carry on getting in trouble. I knew I had to do something different – which is what led me to what is now MacRebur.

I took our household waste plastics to our garage, shredded them and mixed them into various forms. From my limited chemistry background, I knew plastics originally come from the ground. They're engineered from fracked oil – like the stuff that holds a road together. A road is made up of stone aggregates stuck together with a 'glue' of bitumen, which is an oil-based compound. Since they came from the same source, there must be a way to mix plastics into bitumen. It was just a matter of working out the chemistry.

A plastic water bottle is not just a bottle. (Surreal, eh? Like that painting, *This is Not a Pipe*!)

That one bottle contains three different polymers: the bottle, the lid and the wrap with the label on it. What I had to do was to separate those different plastics, mix them back together, trying different percentages of each ingredient to find out what worked and what didn't.

I sent each mix down to a proper accredited asphalt lab and had it tested until I found the right proportions of the right plastics to mix with the right bitumen so that they mixed together and didn't cause all sorts of problems. It took 844 failed test results and eighteen months – but the 845th mixture worked. I applied for a patent, talked a couple of friends into the idea and we were in business.

In essence, what I was doing wasn't anything new. There are roads all over the world made of the same stuff: asphalt (the mix of bitumen and stones). I wasn't trying to make a better road; I was simply trying to replicate roads that already existed. The difference was, I was doing so by using waste plastics.

One of my grandmother's sayings has always stuck with me: 'Toby, there is money in old muck'.

You can make money from the rubbish people throw away.

I knew there must have been a way to take these two global problems – the plastic epidemic on one side and the poor quality of roads on the other – and solve both with one simple solution.

I knew if I stuck with it long enough, I would find the solution. I kept the Colonel Sanders story in my mind: his recipe for Kentucky fried chicken was rejected 1,009 times before it got accepted.

In my view, entrepreneurship has to be a labour of love.

To this day, I've never created a business model or a business plan; I've created pitch decks. For me, it's all about taking a problem, adding it to something I'm passionate about – and never giving up. I knew I had to make my plastic-road idea work. It cost my colleagues and I a fortune for each test we put the product through. But the 845th result made it all worthwhile.

The Rag and Bone Man

As I've mentioned, when I was home from boarding school, I used to spend time with my grandparents at Morecambe Bay in Lancashire, UK.

Every Tuesday, Dougie Ruth used to come around to my grandparents' house on a horse and cart and ring a bell, just as we were about to have tea. He was the rag and bone man. There were rag and bone men all over the country. They collected old stuff.

My grandparents used to go out with metal objects: old toasters and kettles, you name it. Any old metal people didn't want any more, they would give to Dougie. He would recycle and fix up the old toasters and things and sell them to people cheaper than they could buy them in the shops. The rag and bone men were the first real recyclers. What couldn't be resold, they would melt down and sell as jewellery and other things. They were always paid in cash.

Dougie's horse knew the area so well that, after Dougie enjoyed his time at the local pub, the horse would pull him back home.

One summer when I was about twelve, Dougie died. His old gypsy caravan held millions of pounds in cash. Dougie had been one of the wealthiest people in Morecambe Bay.

That was my first real experience of turning old muck into money. It had a profound impact on me because it was the first example of taking things that people threw away and turning them into something of value. For me, that was a paradigm shift from what I thought people in business were doing versus what business actually is.

I was familiar with having something worth money and selling it to other people. But taking something with apparently no value and turning it into something worth money: that is the real power of an entrepreneur, rather than just being the middleman in a deal, like a shopkeeper. If you think about the greatest businesses, they have invented a concept or created something from nothing.

The Rag and Bone Man stuck with me for years. I became fascinated by entrepreneurialism that can turn nothing into something. When I originally had the idea of putting waste plastics into roads, I got in touch with the co-founder of another business doing just that.

In 2013, student Arthur Kay noticed a film of what appeared to be oil collecting on his cold Americano, so he started to research if used coffee grounds contain oil, and if they could therefore be used as a fuel source. It turns out that they did – and they could. He went on to establish a new business, Bio-Bean, that develops coffee-derived biomass pellets. He launched coffee collection services across the UK and, by 2015, had built the world's first industrial-scale coffee-recycling factory.

Bio-Bean has since launched its first consumer retail product, Coffee Logs, and its first natural flavour ingredient for the food and beverage industry. Today, the company is the UK's largest recycler of coffee grounds, with the support of an award-winning team of 30, working with some of the biggest companies in the country to transform coffee waste into valuable products on an industrial scale.

It's businesses like Bio-Bean that I believe will thrive, despite any pandemic or financial depression. There's always a place for businesses that can solve multiple world problems with simple solutions.

Mindset Exercise: Mind Flexibility Equals Growth

The word 'mindset' is an oxymoron. (In Chapter Eighteen, you'll learn about the benefit of not having your mind *set* at all, but instead having flexibility.)

In 2008, Kate decided to take a holiday with her friends, without me, as we were planning to have a family and she was preparing to never be allowed out again after the baby was born. Kate wanted a last shindig before the baby arrived. Being traditionally Scottish, Kate is good with her money and had booked the cheapest holiday she could find on the internet. The catch was that the flight left at 4:00 am from Manchester Airport, a good three-hour drive away from our home.

As a good husband, I offered to drive her rather than having her get a taxi at that time in the morning. I also wanted to make sure she caught the flight because I had my mates coming round to watch rugby the next day, and was looking forward to a day without any interruptions. I dropped off Kate for her flight and drove home, excited to get ready for my mates' arrival – and I suspect like most people facing a three-hour drive on an empty road at 4:00 am, I put my foot down and drove over the speed limit. Just a bit.

After about an hour, I saw flashing blue lights in my mirrors and was pulled over by the police. The policeman who got out of the car looked as if he could be the age of my son. He asked me to wind my window down and started talking to me like a child who has been caught doing something naughty in the playground. 'Do you know how fast you were going?' he asked. 'What would you do if a deer ran out in front of you?' I could feel frustration building up and it was all I could do not to respond with: 'I've been driving longer than you've been alive, son, so I think I would know what to do better than you if a bloody deer ran out in front of me.'

He continued to treat me like a child who had no idea what I was doing. Then he asked me the question I'll never forget. 'What would you do, driving over the speed limit into Mr. Fog?'

My temper boiled over. I stared him right in the eyes and said one word at a time, speaking very clearly as if to someone slightly deaf: 'Well, officer. I would put Mr. Foot on Mr. Brake and I would slow Mr. Car down, thank you very much, you jumped up little s**t!'

He calmly took a step back from my car and said in a raised voice, 'Sir, I shall repeat my question. What would you do, driving over the speed limit into MIST or FOG...?'

I had no response. I got my ticket and now drive at the appropriate speed limit wherever I go, night or day.

I completely distorted what the policeman asked me because my mindset was such that I didn't want to hear him properly. I became fixed in a mindset that he was treating me like a child and no matter what he had asked, I was going to get one over him. Or so I thought.

Your mission in this exercise is to think about your business mindset. If you currently operate from a fixed mindset, you can work on changing it to have mind flexibility, because this equals business growth every time.

Our mindset can be described as the way we present, or represent, the world and our place in it to ourselves. It's normal for people to doubt their own abilities, but your doubts become your thoughts and your thoughts become your behaviours – and patterns of behaviour can easily hold you and your business back.

Have you ever caught yourself thinking things like: 'I'd rather die than speak in front of people', 'What's the point in even trying?' or 'I'm not a confident person' and 'I have such a bad memory for names'? These kinds of statements all come from having a fixed mindset and one of the quickest ways to change them is to change your language.

Having mind flexibility will lead you to create a growth mindset. In the words of the U.S. psychologist Carol Dweck, who came up with the concept, a growth mindset is *based on the belief that your basic qualities are things you can cultivate through your efforts*.

When you catch yourself saying 'I'm not good at that!' or 'I give up!' or 'It's too hard', make an effort to change your language. Try adding the word 'yet' at the end of the sentences, so they become 'I'm not good at that, *yet*', or 'I can't do that, *yet*'.

These sentences presuppose you will be able to do whatever it is in time and 'trick' your unconscious mind into believing something different to being fixed in a limiting mindset.

Chapter Ten Principle:

Take a problem, add passion — and don't give up.

No Idea Is Rubbish

IN 2015, WHEN I HAD THE CRAZY IDEA OF USING WASTE PLASTICS TO MAKE our roads more durable and at the same time help stop the epidemic of waste plastic, I decided to enter Sir Richard Branson's Virgin VOOM competition. Branson created it to find budding entrepreneurs with business ideas he would like to invest in. That year, 22,000 businesses entered.

So many people said to me, 'Your idea is rubbish.' (Rubbish, geddit?) They said, 'This will never work. It's too simple. It's never going to happen. You're just a dreamer.'

At the time, it was a brand-new concept, an idea that hadn't been done before, so naturally there were naysayers and haters. Lots of them. Large construction firms said it wouldn't work; many local authorities, plastic recyclers, roads engineers, and even the UK Department of Transport agreed.

I decided to enter the contest anyway, primarily on the off-chance that I might get to meet Branson again. I still had my man-crush on him, so I'd jump at any opportunity to come into contact with him. You know that idea that we become the five people we hang out with? Well, I thought if I could just hang out with Sir Richard enough, I could become more like him.

Out of the thousands of businesses, we got down to the last 80. The quarter finals. I thought, 'This is great!' It was an ego booster. I had to pitch to various people at Virgin to get to the next stage. Would you believe it? I got through to the semi-finals!

I was in the top twenty. I pitched again and got into the finals: the top three. I couldn't believe it! Now I would have a 90-second 'Pitch to Rich', presenting to Sir Richard and some other entrepreneurs he had invited to be on the judge's panel, including Tyra Banks, America's Next Top Model creator and producer, and Sara Blakely, the owner of Spanks.

As I contemplated how to pitch to Tyra Banks, I thought, 'How the hell do I make rubbish, plastics and roads sexy enough that America's Top Model's producer will love what I'm talking about?' I pictured myself in her shoes (not a pretty sight let me tell you): what would I ask myself? The only thing I came up with was that Tyra Banks has a lot of beauty products: perfumes, exfoliation products and such. A lot of those products contain nearly invisible micro-plastics that end up going down the plug when we wash with some products – and into the oceans.

At MacRebur, we take waste plastics and homogenise them with bitumen (oil) so we don't have any micro-plastics. As an analogy, when you open a tin of paint, there is oil sitting on top – but it disappears when you stir it in to make a homogenous mix. That's what we do. We take the plastics and mix them thoroughly into the bitumen to stop the ingredients from separating.

So, when I sat in Tyra Banks' shoes, I imagined her asking me about plastics in bathroom products. And she did. I had prepared a little vial of micro-plastics, which I had in my blazer. I took it out and said, 'Tyra, I think what you're asking about is micro-plastics'. I explained how MacRebur was cleaning them up.

I found out later that she walked up to Richard Branson after my pitch and said, 'Toby McCartney is the winner'. And I was. I won the whole competition.

I had gone from having a crazy idea that everyone apart from my family and friends – and even they took some convincing – had said wouldn't work, to having Sir Richard Branson, who knows a thing or two about business, saying that it would. (In fact, today, the largest asphalt manufacturer in England, whose representatives told me in meeting after meeting that my idea wouldn't work, is now using exactly the process I thought up – FUCM some might say...)

Winning the Virgin VOOM 2016 competition meant that I got to meet Sir Richard Branson several times. I got to go to his home in Oxford and I think I counted six swimming pools on the way into his house; I got invited to Necker, his private island in the British Virgin Islands. I got to have dinner with him, his family and other entrepreneurs I knew the names of and had followed their business journeys. The first thing I did when I got to Richard's house was take a selfie on his toilet. I know, I know. It may be immature, but it just seemed like the thing to do. I was on Richard Branson's bog. I had to take a selfie. (Maybe that's the kind of thing that teacher meant when he wrote in my report about my 'acts of lunacy'.)

One of the main things that surprised me were Sir Richard's family values. He constantly talks about his daughter, Holly, and spends a lot of time with his family. That was a great lesson for me. It's not all about business. When we step outside of the business is when we can think clearly – and why not do so while spending time with family?

Another thing I learned from Sir Richard is that creating a business is not just about creating more financial wealth. It's about creating more time wealth to spend with the people we love. That's something he does exceptionally well.

The experience, once again, underlined the idea that he is just a bloke doing something he loves. I think that's what appealed to him about MacRebur. I was a bloke doing something that I love, too.

You might be wondering if he remembers writing me a letter when I was nine years old. No, sadly. He had some vague recollection of the time we met in Pollensa. But not enough to know who I was.

This was my prize: Branson invested some cash into MacRebur. That's what really got the business started. We went from zero to money in the bank right out of the gate. We hadn't built a single road before the competition and then, suddenly, bang: we got ourselves a unicorn.

Zeroes to heroes

The prize didn't just come in cash. Sir Richard gave us advertising with JCDecaux, the outdoor advertising agency. He put us in touch with a number of investors who are now part of our business. It had taken me 35 years searching for this unicorn, and then in one competition in a single day, I found it. But it had taken everything that happened in my life since I was nine years old to lead me there.

Nothing we do in life or in business is wasted. Lessons are learned, and connections are made that could just lead us to our goal.

In early 2018, MacRebur was valued at £17 million (a far cry from £0 in 2016). We have factories in the United States and have laid roads all over the world. We have a large team of people working from Lockerbie, Scotland, and we are making a dent in the plastic epidemic – even if, for now, it remains just a dent.

We are now starting to see competitors. Other companies are trying to do what we are doing. On one hand, we don't want competitors; on the other, we know we are pioneering a movement when we start seeing people copying our idea. Having competitors is a good thing because there is so much plastic waste to get rid of. Our original mission was, 'Rid the world of the plastic epidemic'. Well, we're not going to do that on our own. The more help the better.

If you reflect back on your life, you will likely see events or circumstances in your personal life or in business that led you to where you are today. Maybe there's a story about how you met your significant other or came to have the idea for the business you are running (or want to run) today. You might also recall events or experiences in your past that seem initially to be negative—to have held you back from where it is you want to go.

If that's the case, try this technique to help you see that every experience holds purpose in your life.

 Mindset Exercise: Turning back the clock

This process is a time-based technique, borrowing resources from today and resources from your guru or an imaginary guru. Everybody in business needs a guru. It might be someone like Sir Richard Branson or someone else you admire. But if you have spotted traits in someone else that you admire, that means you must have them within yourself, too, so you can be your own guru.

This simple technique requires you to imagine going back into the past to the first time you experienced a particular negative emotion, whether it be anger, sadness, fear, or guilt – pick whichever one you feel is holding you back. You are going to go back in an imaginary time machine to that event. However, you're not going to see it from the point of view of the one having the experience but that of your guru. Your guru is going to offer your younger self the advice you need to overcome that negative emotion.

This technique comes from Gestalt Therapy, which, simply put, is a psychotherapeutic approach developed by Fritz Perls that focuses on insight into human gestalts – a gestalt is an organised whole that is perceived as more than the sum of its parts – and their relations to the world. It often uses role playing to aid the resolution of past conflicts. In Gestalt Theory, the memory is like a chain of pearls. If you can get back to the origin, the first pearl, and reframe it, you're cutting the chain. All the other pearls – the negative emotions – drop away.

So, go back to the event you have in mind. Now, disassociate from the experience and become your guru. Your guru is going to offer your younger self advice on what you need to feel differently, how to behave differently, what environment you could change that's different, what values and beliefs you could hold that would help you change that negative emotion and who you really are.

You will realise that this limiting belief or that stress or negative emotion does not serve you in business. Use your new resources to give advice to your younger self and check to see if the negative emotion is still there or if it has disappeared.

If it has not disappeared, go back into the guru position. Offer yourself more advice. If it has disappeared, you can move forward with the new learning, applying it to every time you experienced that negative emotion or that limiting belief or whatever it might be.

Repeat this process as necessary. Every time you need more new learning, take a step off the timeline or step outside yourself. Give yourself more advice until the advice overcomes whatever negative emotion is present. Check that it has disappeared and move forwards until you get back to the present day.

Chapter 11 Principle:

Nothing we do in life or in business is wasted.

CHAPTER TWELVE

The Power of 'Yes'

ONE DAY IN 2011, I WAS IN CARLISLE'S TOWN CENTRE HAVING COFFEE WITH Kate. There was a folk -rock band playing in the square, and I loved them. I went up to the singer afterwards and said, 'I want to buy your CD. Where is it? You didn't pitch it at the end of your set.' She said, 'Oh, we don't have one yet. We just play in local pubs and clubs.'

Now, I'm the sort of person who can't just have a hobby. I turn my hobbies into businesses. When I learned the guitar, I had to sell guitars. When I bought a motor home for holidays, I had to rent it out and earn my money back. And I can't just listen to music I like. I have to do something about it. I said to her, 'Listen, I have zero music experience. Most people would laugh at my music tastes. But I want to manage your band. I think I could get you to number one in the folk-rock charts.'

I'd never even met a musician before. But I made the promise, because I felt confident I could fulfill it.

The singer's name is Fiona Clayton. She said, 'Let me speak to the other band members and I'll get back to you tomorrow.' I gave her my business card, figuring I'd never hear from her again. But she called the next day. 'How would you feel about helping us get an album out there, to see what you can do?' I said, 'Okay, great.'

I got a lawyer to draw up a five-year contract and I said to the band: 'Here's the deal. This is a five-year contract. Any money that you make, I take my cut, but within the first year, if I can't get you an album and get you to the number one slot of the folk-rock charts, then the contract is null and void.' They thought it was brilliant, so we signed the deal.

I was a band manager.

I started working on my mission straightaway. I found a studio and called some contacts I had that might have vaguely known somebody in the music business, and I booked them time. I got the band into the studio and we started to record. About six months later, they had an album of their own songs, *As I Dive In*. Then I got a designer to design the album cover. It was like being a music production company.

My next task was to get them to the number one slot. I booked a venue and planned a launch party. I got everybody I've ever known to come along to hear the band play a gig. My friends supported the band by buying some albums. I then got the album onto Amazon and I managed to convince the staff of our local music shop to place the album right at the front.

A week after we released the album, it got to number one in the folk-rock charts. And the first single we took from the album, "Fearless," the track that we wanted everybody to listen to, got to number one on the HMV chart, a worldwide chart for folk rock. It also got to number 140 in the BBC pop charts.

Fiona now tours all around the world with her band, but her number-one album was created by me and my made-up record label – and all because I believed that anything in business is possible, even with no experience. What it took was passion. I loved Fiona's music and willed it to succeed. After reaching my goal one year into the five-year contract, we parted ways. My intention was never to go into the music business; I just wanted to have the band record an album and get to number one.

The principle here is: Believe in yourself, believe in your product.

A great product you believe in can get you a long way, regardless of whether you know what you're doing. There's so much indecision out there; I encourage budding entrepreneurs to just say 'yes' to an opportunity, and then figure out how to make it work.

If you are looking to build a business, some of the best advice I can give you is to not let your identity become attached to its outcome or success. People sometimes get stuck with the mindset, 'If this fails, then I am a failure. What are people going to think?' I just try everything that I fancy, with this mindset: 'This was something I believed in. I accomplished it, or I didn't. Either way, I had fun and I'm onto something else.'

Since many people struggle with limiting beliefs when it comes to believing in themselves and their goals, this is a technique I like to use with my clients to build empowerment.

 Mindset Exercise: The Belief Change

This exercise is useful when you want to change a limiting belief that would stop you from becoming a successful entrepreneur. It is divided into four steps.

Step One: Assess a Current Limiting Belief

Let's say the limiting belief is, *I'm not good enough to start my own business.*

1. Think about what pictures come to mind when you think that belief.
2. Ask yourself, *What feelings are present when I think about that limiting belief?*
3. Think about sounds. Are there any sounds that are important to you when you think about that limiting belief?

4. Write down what pictures, sounds and feelings come to mind.

5. Mentally 'clear the screen'. Think about something – anything – completely different.

Step Two: Assess a Belief That Is No Longer True

Next, think about a belief that is no longer true for you. It used to be true, no longer. This could be anything from, *I believe I'll never have children*, or *I believe I'll never be happy*, or *I believe I'll never find a partner*, *I'll never be able to drive*, *I'll never get any qualifications*. Whatever it is for you. For me, for example, the belief *I'll never get any qualifications* was true when I was at school but no longer. As you did in Step One, think about and write down what pictures, sounds and feelings come to mind, this time from the belief that is no longer true. My inner coding of that belief is now different, because I have proved to myself that that belief is no longer true.

Step Three: Map across the pictures, sounds and feelings

Now, swap the pictures, sounds and feelings from the belief that is no longer true onto the belief that limits you. If the pictures are different or the sounds are louder or there is different music playing, or if the feelings are in a different place or one is warm and one is cold, for example, swap them. You should be thinking of the belief that limits you, but now with the pictures, sounds and feelings of the belief that used to be true for you but is now no longer true.

Step Four: A Belief That is Absolutely True

Next, think about a belief that is absolutely true for you today. Let's say, *I love my daughters.* No one on the planet could tell me otherwise or prove that I don't because it is simply true. It is a belief I have that is 100% there.

Or, it might be that you love your partner, or you believe that you can run 100 metres in 20 seconds or whatever it might be – but it must be absolutely true for you. You know it's true today and no one could ever prove it wrong. Think of the pictures, sounds and feelings of the belief that is absolutely true. Really associate into this belief.

Step Five: What Belief Would You Like to Have?
Now think about a belief you would like to be true, one that will serve you and is opposite to the limiting belief you thought of in Step One. If the belief in Step One was, *I'm not good enough to go into business*, the opposing belief here could be, *I am confident in business and I'm going to make a success of my business*.

Think about the inner coding of this desirable belief. What would it be like to believe you are confident? What pictures, sounds and feelings would you have? Think about that new belief with the inner coding of a belief that is absolutely true for you. So, take the same pictures, the same sounds and the same feelings that you get from knowing you love your daughters or your spouse and then think about the new belief with that inner coding.

It takes some practice, but this technique should change the way you feel about any limiting belief. This is a way of turning a limiting belief into an empowering belief.

Chapter 12 Principle:

Believe in yourself, believe in your product.

Free Your Mind

ANYONE FACING A DECISION CAN FEEL CONFLICTED. IT'S AS IF WE WERE SPLIT into more than one person, with two voices in our heads. Those voices lead to indecision and conflict. I notice this conflict all the time when I'm selling from the room. If I'm running a training course, I say, 'Here's the programme. This is how much it costs. Fill in a booking form if you'd like to book.' For the rest of the day, I can see people running scenarios through their heads: 'I'd like to book, but maybe I can't afford it', or 'I'd like to do it, but I don't know if I've got the time', or 'I'd like to do it, but I'm worried that this isn't the right programme for me.' Indecision stops them in their tracks and consumes their energy.

If they don't book, there will be downsides. They're going to miss out on the rest of the training. If they do book, there are a lot of upsides, of course, but there are also downsides, because they are going to have to spend the money, invest the time and so on. All of those considerations are real. But once they've decided to either book or not book, the conflict is resolved. That frees their mind to think about learning and growing, rather than the conflict.

This applies to all decisions. If I'm trying to decide, 'Should I start my business, or should I stay at work and keep the stability that a salary provides?'

With both decisions, there is a deeper question to consider.

I have a client who works in a dead-end job. He doesn't like it, but he continues to stay there because it pays the bills. However, he is not motivated while at work; he starts a task and gets waylaid. He is considering starting a business to get out of his job. But here's the catch. Starting a business isn't an alternative to getting a job or staying in a job you don't like. You start a business because you're passionate about something and you want to have that as a business.

Like the book title says, it's a Business ReLOVEution.

Starting a business should be about moving *towards* your passion and purpose, not away from the pain of something you hate. Many people see the decision as either/or, but that's not in favour of your highest good. 'Either/or' thinking can trick us into indecision.

When we're undecided, we hold ourselves back from any change at all. It's important to be aware that there are going to be upsides and downsides to any decision we make, but indecision only perpetuates the downsides of your current situation. Make a decision and then live with the good and the bad that comes with it. You'll be able to move on – and you can always make a different decision later.

Often when people come to me and say, 'Part of me really wants to start this business, and part of me just wants to stay at work because I've got security with my work and consistent money', I take a coin from my pocket. I say, 'Okay, let's say heads is that you give up work and start your own business, and tails is that you stay at work.' And then I ask, 'Heads or tails?' I always trust what they say, their unconscious response. Whichever side they pick, I recommend they go with that decision. I don't need to flip the coin. It's not about the flip of a coin. It's about their unconscious decision.

I don't think there's any successful entrepreneur that takes a long time to make decisions, because the longer we take, the more opportunities we miss out on. Make an informed decision, knowing and being comfortable with the negatives and, of course, the positives.

U.S. President Harry S. Truman liked to say, 'Imperfect action always beats perfect inaction.'

People often wait for things to be perfect; they wait for the perfect moment to make a decision and it never comes. It's never there. We have to make decisions in imperfect moments. As entrepreneurs, we have to be comfortable with sometimes being uncomfortable. Decisions we have to make aren't always easy, but we have to make them nevertheless.

Sometimes, getting space away from the decisions you have to make every day is important. I find it so valuable to find sanctuary as often as I can, away from the business and the 'busy-ness' of it all. Often, I find that the answer to a decision comes to me when I'm in my place of sanctuary.

Find the Right Environment

I believe every entrepreneur should have a sanctuary of some sort. Sometimes you can use mindful practices to find your sanctuary in the moment. In addition to those mindful practices, it is also worth having a hobby or a sport or a place that is completely separate from the business you are creating.

My sanctuary is a villa in Turkey. I can go there and be completely removed from business or the politics of life. My family – my two girls and my wife – have time to relax and think. I come up with my best ideas there.

You don't necessarily need a villa in Turkey. My friend Hayley lives in Australia, where she teaches children life skills such as confidence and financial awareness. She lives right by the beach, and every morning she goes for a jog with her daughter. She says that is where she comes up with the most innovative ideas, new concepts and products and services for her business. This is her sanctuary.

Another client of mine, David, uses sports as a means to mentally and physically retreat from the pressures of his work life. He plays a lot of squash, and says it frees his mind from the business world. Nick, my MacRebur co-director, goes to the gym every morning at 6:00 am. His rule is to not think about anything business-related while he is there. The gym is his sanctuary.

You can create a sanctuary just about anywhere. And if you can't find a physical place, take up a hobby or sport, anything that is completely separate from your business, and that will take your mind off your day-to-day concerns. You can also be clever and include your family and friends so that you spend more time with them doing something that is not business-related. As an added bonus, it helps you to stop talking only about business all the time. 'All work and no play', as the saying goes.

If you really aren't able to remove yourself physically from the concerns of business, here is a mindset technique to help you find a sanctuary in your mind.

 Mindset Exercise – Find Your Sanctuary

This technique gives us a way to break through an unwanted negative state that seemingly can't be shaken off. Instead, it allows us to find a resourceful positive state that will enable us to live a life full of possibility and positivity.

Sometimes a negative state overwhelms us and we can become stuck in a rut. We know that the negative state we experience isn't serving us, but we have lost the ability to find an alternative. Sanctuary allows us to take back control and move ourselves into being at ease with personal empowerment. Many people experience overwhelm, anxiety, stress and depression, especially at times of such great uncertainty in the world.

Sanctuary is a technique taught on our courses, designed by John Grinder and Carmen Bostic St Clair. It combines NLP anchoring and collapsing anchors with perceptual positions.

These are the steps we take to help ourselves feel differently about those overwhelming negative emotions that sometimes overpower us:

1. **Position 1:** From a dissociated position, create a visual and auditory representation of yourself with the negative overwhelming state/s. Notice your environment and behaviours in that moment and imagine your beliefs and values in that moment, too. Discover what might trigger that state (what happens just before you experience that negative state) and notice what patterns are present in your behaviours in that moment. Make sure you are dissociated from that position, so you can see yourself in it and are not looking through your own eyes.

2. **Position 2:** Now locate a 'sanctuary' position separate from position 1, approximately two to five metres away. Imagine building your sanctuary as the most positive place you can possibly create. Become childlike with your imagination, add in colours to your pictures, make things bigger and brighter if that helps, think of music or bird song you would like to add, and find as many positive resources (positive emotions) you would like to have in your sanctuary: happiness, joy, kindness, compassion, confidence, positivity, excitement and so on. Make sure you only have extremely positive resources in Position 2. Once you're happy with your sanctuary make sure you lock it into the position you have imagined for Position 2 (some people imagine a bubble around it or an acrylic screen surrounding it, so that all of that positivity cannot escape).

Now you have two spaces marked out on in front of you. One is a negative space, and the other is your sanctuary.

3. Now step inside your sanctuary (associate). Build it by intensifying the visual, auditory and kinaesthetic emotions and surround yourself with as much positivity you can find from your imagination. Fully associate and make sure it's a 10/10 for positivity: the best place on Earth. If it's not, rework your imagined Position 2 until it is.
4. Now step out of your sanctuary into a new position situated next to your sanctuary, but reassociate into an everyday feeling (neutral ground). Let's call this Position 3. Understand that your sanctuary position is just to one side of you, should you need to jump back into total positivity and resourcefulness at any time.
5. In Position 3, walk *slowly* towards the old unwanted state (Position 1), but as you get closer, if at any point you feel any slight degree of negativity, immediately jump into your sanctuary. Keep stepping in and out of sanctuary as you feel you need it until you can step into Position 1 and be comfortable there, too.

It's important to note that you are not walking towards Position 1 whilst in your sanctuary. As soon as you detect any negative kinesthetic whilst in Position 3, you can jump into the positivity contained within your sanctuary. If you walk with the resources activated, you will not be sensitised to the earlier trigger of the unwanted state contained within Position 1.

Chapter 13 Principle:

Indecision is not an option.

CHAPTER FOURTEEN

Reverse Shoplifting

Sometimes, being an entrepreneur is like being a detective; you have to solve apparently unsolvable problems.

In 2008, I decided to write and self-publish a book, *Mastering Memory*, about various memory techniques, which is something I'm passionate about. I published it as an e-book, but then thought, 'I'd like to get this book into the shops'.

Online, all the advice was that I had to find a traditional publisher in order to get my book into book shops. I believed that, but I didn't want to believe it. I figured there must be another way.

Cue my inner Sherlock Holmes.

I stuck with self-publishing. I used a print-on-demand printing company, got the book onto Amazon and ordered print copies for my friends, family and colleagues. I got a lot of positive feedback, which was good for my ego – but that wasn't enough. I wanted to go into bookstores all over the world and see my book. But I was told again: 'There's no way your book's getting into the shops without a publisher.'

I'd written to a number of publishers and been rejected. To be honest, the book was awful. It was just a set of tools and techniques, so no wonder no-one wanted to publish it. That wasn't important. What was important was that I didn't want to believe that I needed a publisher, because I knew I wouldn't find one.

That was the unsolvable problem. My solution was what I call 'reverse shoplifting'.

Reverse Shoplifting

I printed my book with its own ISBN code on the back; that's the long code that identifies every book in the world in the publishing trade. I ordered 20 copies and sent them with a letter to 20 of my friends, along with a £20 note. The letter read, 'Dear friend, please take my book to your local bookstore. Browse around the books, then go up to the cashier's desk with this copy of my book and use the enclosed 20-pound note to buy it.'

The cashier scanned the barcode and took the money. But because my book wasn't in their system, of course, the system would set up an alert that the title was 'Out of stock'. Once that happened, it automatically ordered five copies of my book (or at least, that's how it worked at the time). Every store in which my friends 'bought' the book would soon have five copies in stock. That is how I got my self-published book into bookshops wherever I had friends. The bookshop got money for nothing, and I got what I wanted: my book on their shelves.

I'm always a little bit embarrassed when I share that story. It is not a strategy I recommend. But I can't help being also a little proud. It's an example of thinking outside the box: reverse engineering, if you will.

Entrepreneurs should always look to overcome the obstacles that are inevitably always thrown at them. There is always a way. Become a detective, and you will find it.

Modern Day Disruptors

Need some more examples of companies that thought outside the box? Here are three companies that detected a problem – from the need to move away from fossil fuels to the barrier of finding a time and place to exercise – and came up with innovative solutions.

I love technology. I buy every gadget I can to help me save time and reduce effort. My most recent purchase, and a real disruptor of transportation, was a Jaguar iPace Electric Car – and I love it. I sat down and worked out how much I could save by driving electric rather than my old diesel car. My annual motoring bills have been reduced from £500 to £50 per month. There are tax breaks, incentive schemes, grants and offers available to anyone who wants to convert to electric.

I also love another motoring disruptor, Rivian. Rivian has made a name for itself by building electric pickup trucks and SUVs, vehicles usually identified with rugged, diesel-loving builder folks. Even though it hasn't yet released its first model to the public, Rivian's technology is so promising that it is valued at more than $1 billion and has attracted Ford and Amazon as investors.

On the exercise front, Peloton has disrupted the fitness industry. Based in New York City, the company sells high-end stationary bikes and treadmills, and offers live-streamed boot-camp, strength training, yoga and cardio classes that make it easy for members to work out in their own homes at the times they choose. 2020 was a transformative year for Peleton, which crushed revenue estimates, reporting triple digit increases in Q4 of 2020. Their estimated revenue was $700 million but their total actual revenue for the 2020 fiscal year was $1.8 billion.[8]

What about You?

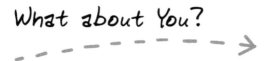

Here are a few principles I've used with my own businesses that can help you disrupt and innovate, too:

- **Ask 'What would I like to happen next?, 'How can I make this better?' and 'What if (plus)?':** We're in a new age of disrupting business for good, where whole industries are being transformed and changed for the better. Amazon is reshaping the way we buy our products. Electric vehicles are changing the way we get around.
- Henry Ford is famous for his (possibly dubious) quote, "If I had asked the people what they wanted, they would have said faster horses." Don't count on the status quo to remain the status quo, because the status quo is something of the past!
- **Combine purpose and profit:** Your business must be driven by purpose – some sort of environmental or social cause. If you live and work with purpose, profit will follow.
- **Embrace your own disruption:** Continually disrupt for good. Look for ways to expand your skills and improve your products and services. Take what already exists and make it better. Don't be afraid to scrap a business model for a fresh approach. Be agile.
- **Stay focused on solving client issues:** As your business grows, operations will get more complex. Resist the urge to get pulled into internal politics, struggles and issues. Stay focused on serving your clients. Find out what's important to them and do everything you can to deliver it.

- **Treat your staff well:** Your biggest asset will be your staff. Make it your mission to provide your staff members with benefits that meet their top values. Make sure your staff are happy, and productivity will go up.
- **Find partners who share your vision and value your business:** Find partners that serve your needs, too. Don't settle for sub-par service because you're a small business. There are plenty of companies that want your business and can support your growth.

The pandemic of 2020 saw the world change. Everything is different. You see the future as either daunting or exciting. Either way, the new conditions created an abundance of opportunities for small businesses in almost every field. The survivors are those that reinvent themselves and don't just count on surviving but find new ways of thriving.

Chapter 14 Principle:

There is always a solution. Become a detective, and you will find it.

Don't Be Like Phil

OF ALL THE MARKETING TOOLS AND TECHNIQUES OUT THERE, FROM SOCIAL media marketing, running webinars, distributing brochures, phone advertising and so on, the best tool I've ever found is to speak from a stage. Public-speaking skills are the most important tool in the entrepreneur's toolbox.

If you're going into business, there are five phases every successful entrepreneur goes through in order to attract customers or clients. These are taken from John Jantsch's book, *Duct Tape Marketing*, and I find them incredibly useful:

1. Know – Let people get to know you
2. Like – Get people to like you
3. Trust – Gain people's trust
4. Buy – Once people know, like and trust you, they will likely buy from you
5. Refer – If you have accomplished all of the above, your customers or clients are likely to refer you to others

Kate and I have created every business we have by following these five principles. They're the core of every business decision, whether it be how much to spend on marketing, how long to give something away for free, whether to include social-media marketing in your business or whether to rent an office. Every decision is based on whether it helps customers get to Know, Like, Trust, Buy or Refer you. If it does, we do it. If it doesn't, we forget it.

It really is that simple.

Jantsch's first three phases are where marketing comes in. I achieved all of them by going up on stage and telling stories about myself that are interesting and relatable, which I learned how to do by taking public speaking programmes.

How will you get your story out?

You don't need to be a public speaker to tell a good story, but it helps.

Phil came to one of our intensives in Scotland. Everyone *loved* Phil, a friendly, likeable management consultant from Yorkshire who was a joy to work with. If you spent a long time with Phil, your jaw ached from smiling! Phil wasn't just a nice guy. We started to realise that he was also an excellent coach and was taking to NLP training like a duck to water. He was Mr. Rapport and the students who worked with him gave him glowing feedback.

Phil happened to mention one day that he had started his own coaching business. We were happy for him because it was a great career choice, and later that day we invited him up to the front of the small group. He sat on a stool next to us and was easy and comfortable, making jokes and clearly enjoying himself. But then something unexpected happened.

We asked him to tell us about his new coaching business, which was his chance to sell his skills to a room full of people. Instantly, all his warmth and authenticity left the room. In fact, it left the whole building. Phil morphed into some weird *robot* blurting out the benefits of coaching as if he was reading them from a management training book from the eighties.

We've had a *lot* of 'Phil experiences' over the years. There seems to be a sudden disconnect when people get on stage. Maybe it's an anchor to the word 'business' or 'selling', but people screw up.

It doesn't have to be that way. All a potential client wants is *you*, doing the thing you're good at, to help them. That's all anyone wanted from Phil – for him to just keep being himself, because that was already enough. What Phil hadn't learnt was that it's not so much about how *he* feels on stage – whether or not he's nervous, or hating every second; it's about the experience the people in the audience have. That's why a story is such a powerful thing, because people like stories. Once I realised that, it made me feel a lot more comfortable on stage. Once I understood the importance of stories, and I figured out the way I want to tell each one, I found that I earned people's trust – which meant they would buy from me.

Exercise: Stories for Telling...

We want to help you overcome this disconnect between how you feel and your ability to share what you do. And we are going to do that by working on knowing what your message is and learning how to communicate it to the world.

Find *your* message and communicate it so you can find and impress on *your* people:

1. First, think back to what has brought you on this journey and what you have learnt about yourself.
2. Be open and vulnerable with your own change, as that helps your clients do the same.

3. It's OK to be totally honest; in fact, it's a must. Your clients don't want to work with someone who has *everything* perfectly worked out. They want to follow a person who struggles the same way they do, but who is still willing to push forward. This gives them hope to be able to do the same.
4. Why is the thing you are providing or selling uniquely connected to you?

Humans are Hardwired to Remember Stories

One of the greatest skills I ever learnt was to tell a good story. In a book about the modern entrepreneur, storytelling may seem like an outdated tool – and it is. That's exactly what makes it so powerful. A story can capture our imagination and our hearts. Being able to tell a story to the press, and to the public, and learning how to speak to the camera is what got MacRebur's foot in the door. The press absolutely loved the story of how the company was created.

That was a moment I thought, *Thank God for those public speaking skills.*

So many non storytellers just give facts and statistics. They're fine, but they're not really inspirational. They can make a persuasive argument, but they can't bring your vision alive so that people are desperate to buy into it.

The press loved that I was a guy with no school qualifications who got the idea for the business at my daughter's school assembly. My public-speaking skills allowed me to tell the company story and make it engaging. The media – like everyone – want to be entertained.

I don't just speak to people about what I do from a stage or through the media. I speak to everyone I meet about whatever I'm passionate about. Humans find stories irresistible. It's a great way to sell, although I never consciously think that at the time. Instead, I think, 'If I am passionate about a topic, there are bound to be other people that are passionate about it, too – or at least curious about it.' One of the greatest compliments I have ever received was something Richard Branson posted on his Twitter feed: 'Speaking to Toby McCartney about plastic roads really interests me. And if it interests me, it's going to interest many other people that will help their business succeed.'

Lisa Cron, a story analyst, speaker, UCLA instructor and author of *Wired for Story* says, 'When you're lost in a good story, it's not arbitrary, it's not pleasure for pleasure's sake. It's biological, it's chemical, it's a survival mechanism.'

Many business people have already discovered the power a story has to inspire others to action.

Keith Quesenberry, a researcher at Johns Hopkin University, argues that humans are social creatures and stories are how we relate to other people: 'We humans have been communicating through stories for upwards of 20,000 years, back when all we had were cave walls'. When we hear the ending of a story, a satisfactory conclusion, the brain gives us a physical reward by releasing dopamine, a chemical that makes us feel more positive. [9]

In our mindset work, Kate and I discovered long ago that we can tell our brains whatever stories we want and they will believe it. Our brains do not know the difference between truth and fiction – which is precisely why we choose to tell ourselves inspiring, successful stories. The most up-to-date scientific research underlines the importance of stories in changing our behaviours and attitudes – which is why stories are so important to business, where everything we do is designed to influence our clients' decisions. [10]

Paul J. Zak, founding director of the Center for Neuroeconomics Studies and a professor of economics, psychology and management at Claremont Graduate University, carried out experiments that showed that a speaker who uses emotional, character-driven stories is better understood than one who doesn't – and that their points can be remembered weeks later.

You might not remember the exact details of the Five Principles of Success from earlier in this chapter, for example, but I'm willing to bet that you will remember at least one of the stories you've read in this book: the story of negotiating with the Russians, or how I kept bullies at bay with a tuck box, or the time I met Richard Branson in Mallorca.

When a customer likes what they buy, they refer what I'm selling to others. The interesting thing is that they do so by telling my story again, as if it was theirs. And that gets me another customer. Sharing your message with others and learning public speaking skills are key to starting a business.

Here are some tips on how to sound and look like a professional public speaker:

1. Use humour. A big part of public speaking is to be an entertainer. There are plenty of public speakers that don't use humour; that's just my trick. You don't always have to entertain through humour; if that's not your thing, don't use it. The idea is to get a reaction, bring real emotion out of people. The art is to bring both drama and humour into your stories
2. Tell stories – Make A Point, Tell A Story (MAPTAS)
3. Remember to include the 'Three Ps' with each story you tell – Premise, Problem and Payoff:
   a. Premise: What the story is about
   b. Problem: What problem needs to be overcome
   c. Payoff: Solving that problem
4. Keep your feet under your shoulders … never put that leg out.
5. Keep your arms at 90 degrees and hold on to one of your fingers.
6. Use both the pilot's voice (intonate down at the end of your sentences) and the flight attendant's voice (intonate up at the end of your sentences). The pilot sends information, the flight attendant asks questions.

7. Visualise yourself successful. See yourself at the end of the speech surrounded by people asking questions; imagine the applause.

8. Pause, scan, nod and whisper when you deliver key points. Pick out key points of your speech and practice the pause, scan, nod and whisper technique. You can find out more about this on my website below.

9. Breathe low. High breathers make an audience feel nervous. Low breathers help an audience feel relaxed.

10. Close your mouth after every sentence: it will make you look more intelligent. If you keep your mouth open after the full stop, you will lose credibility from your message.

11. Pause between sentences. It will enable the audience to feel like you are in control and give you more credibility. A lot can be said within the pauses.

> Since this isn't a book on public speaking, you can find more information on how to speak like a professional at:
> **www.tobymccartney.com/businessReLOVEution**

Mindset Exercise:
Overcoming Anxiety and Worry

Let's say you have a presentation, a pitch or some form of a public speech coming up. You may be anxious about failing or worrying about whether you are going to be a success.

A simple technique to overcome this is to imagine coming out of your body and floating into the future, 15 minutes after the successful resolution of that speaking engagement or event. Picture yourself looking down through your own eyes,

15 minutes after you have successfully resolved the source of your anxiety or worry.

Realise that you feel very differently 15 minutes after the event. You will probably feel calmer or even be delighted with your performance. Remember that you're visualising the *successful* resolution of whatever the task is. Imagine being in that position, looking through your own eyes, and take the feelings from that future and pump them into your body so they are fully present in the current moment.

Come back to the present. Looking through your own eyes in this very moment, think differently and with different feelings about the presentation that is coming up. This is a quick way to resolve anxiety.

Breathing Techniques

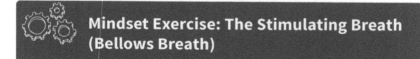

Another way to release anxiety is to be mindful of your breathing. The lower your breath, the less anxious you become. If you feel anxious, worried or nervous about something that is coming up in the future, like starting a business, simply focus your attention on moving your breathing down into the bottom of your belly.

Mindset Exercise: The Stimulating Breath (Bellows Breath)

The stimulating breath or bellows breath is a great way to boost your energy. This type of breathing practice is often done in yoga to help increase Prana, or life force energy.

Stimulating breath can help you increase your energy and help you be more alert. The bellows breath is a safe practice, but it might initially make you dizzy until your body gets used to the increased energy.

Start off by doing the exercise for no longer than 15 seconds, but eventually work up to a minute. Each time you practise this breath, you can increase your time little by little.

1. Sit up tall with your back straight and relax your shoulders.
2. Begin inhaling and exhaling rapidly through your nose. Keep your mouth closed but relaxed. The in and out breaths should be equal in duration, but as short and quick as possible. Be warned: this is a *noisy* breathing exercise.
3. Try for three complete breath cycles per second. As you breathe, you will notice a quick movement of the diaphragm, like a bellows.

This technique should leave you feeling invigorated and alert.

For access to a video demonstrating all these public speaking points, please visit:
www.tobymccartney.com/businessReLOVEution

Chapter 15 Principle:

Invest in learning how to speak like a professional.

Find Your Durmus

I'M NOT SHY ABOUT ASKING PEOPLE FOR HELP. IT MUST BE HUMAN NATURE, but when someone comes to me and says, 'Can you help?' it feels like an honour that they think I can help them. So I love to ask people, 'Can you help me?' Nine times out of ten, they say, 'Yeah, I'll do my best, I'll see what I can do', or 'I might not be able to help you, but I know somebody who can'.

The more you talk about what you do and what you need – especially when you're part of a business ReLOVEution – the more people will want to help. Everybody who starts a business has someone in their list of friends or family or colleagues who can help. Don't be afraid. Ask for help.

The chances are your friends will feel proud if they are able to help you in some way. I have a dear friend in Turkey named Durmus Yeter. He is an entrepreneur in his own right. He earns all of his money in commissions and a small salary from my wife and me as a caretaker for our villa. He tends our pool, services our car, looks after our quad bike and does various other jobs around the villa.

If there is ever anything we need, we ask Durmus for help. He translates for us, and so much more. If we can't get hold of something, he will know how to find it. He will know someone who knows someone. There is always a cousin of his who has what we need. We can ask him for anything. And he loves to be asked – not just from a financial perspective, but because he is a helper. That is his identity.

To give you an example, my daughter plays the saxophone, but on one trip we forgot to bring it with us. We asked Durmus. He knew somebody, one of his cousins or perhaps his cousin's friend, who had a music shop in a town not too far away. He drove us there, and we bought a new saxophone. Durmus earned a commission, and we got what we needed. Everyone knows someone like Durmus. If you don't, my recommendation for all new entrepreneurs is to find one. So many people are frightened to ask for help, but when we start out, asking for help is a necessity.

You'll need help throughout your business journey.

 Exercise: Find Your Tribe

Create a spreadsheet and list your top 10 friends in the first column. In the next column, write down how you think each person on that list might be able to help you in the business. If they can't help you, do they know someone in their network who might be able to help?

No one can do this alone. I have never known a business to be able to function without finding help from other people.

Chapter 16 Principle:

You don't have to do this alone.

EXERCISE: FIND YOUR TRIBE

1. List your **Top 3 needs in business**. What outcome do you want?

2. Create a spreadsheet and list your **top 10 friends** in the first column. Who you will list will vary depending on your answer to Question 1.

3. In the next column, write down how you think each person on that list will be able to help you in the business. If they can't help you, do they know someone in their network that may be able to help?

Top 3 Needs/Outcomes

1.
2.
3.

Top 10 Friends	How Can They Help Me
[Insert Name]	Examples:
1.	• Can they refer me to a new client?
2.	• Do they have an idea (business or otherwise) that will help me grow?
3.	
4.	• Do they have advice/coaching/knowledge that can benefit me?
5.	• Can they invest in my business or send me to investors?
6.	
7.	• Are they able to offer me one of their products or services?
8.	• Barter?
9.	• Share about me on social media?
10.	• Other?

Funding the Dream

WHEN WE STARTED MACREBUR IN 2015, BEFORE THE VOOM COMPETI-tion, we realised early on that the £40,000 my business partners and I each put in was not going to be enough. We were spending so much money on testing our product to find the right mix of plastics that we had nothing left for marketing or to rent an office. We needed to raise capital – and quickly.

Taking what I'd learned about public speaking, I pitched to various venture capitalists (VCs), looking for investors. Although the pitches went well, I wasn't impressed with the questions the VCs asked. They'd often say, 'Why don't you just put new plastics into the roads?' I thought, *You've missed the point. It's a green business, built around taking waste plastics.*

The VCs would talk about the huge sum of money they were expecting our company to be worth. I suppose my understanding of money just wasn't big enough. When people started talking about the company being worth hundreds of millions (one investor said it would be worth £300 million), I remember thinking that wasn't even a real number. It was inconceivable. It was such a huge figure, it didn't mean anything to me. I thought he had made the number up.

We decided not to go with the VCs. It just didn't feel like the right way for us. Instead, I looked into the idea of crowdfunding.

Crowdfunding is King

Traditionally, crowdfunding is based around the principal of buyers 'pre-buying' a product a business is developing. But we didn't have a product as such: there are not many people who want to buy a plastic road. We were more about selling a concept.

We went down the equity-based crowdfunding route, which meant pitching our idea at public events, where we offered the audience the opportunity to invest in MacRebur by buying shares in the business. We used a crowdfunding platform called Seedrs, which functions almost like a competition. The platform gives users 60 days to raise the money they say they need. Otherwise, they get nothing.

We'd worked out that to set up a factory, buy our machinery and everything else, we needed £590,000. It was a huge sum of money. And we had just 60 days. I didn't think I knew enough people to raise that kind of capital in such a short time.

But I tried. I hit the road (pun intended), and pitched at various places around the UK.

When I say I pitched, I mean I told the story. I could hardly pitch the business's success, because we hadn't made a single road. Instead, I told the stories I've told in this book: how my little girl's statement that 'Plastics live in our oceans' inspired me. How I'd seen pickers in India turning plastics into products. How I'd gotten into trouble for putting plastics into potholes.

We then gave audience members the opportunity to invest from £50 up to £500,000. Within 10 days, I'd raised £1.2 million.

But we didn't stop there. Within 15 days, we'd raised nearly £2 million. And we did stop *there*. The figure terrified us. We realised then how valuable our shares in the company were. The more money we raised, the more shares we were giving away. Not wanting to give too much of our company away to investors, we decided to end the first round of fundraising. With 2,000 people believing enough in what we were doing to invest in the company, we figured we had a successful business on our hands.

When we came to the second round of funding the following year, I didn't even bother with pitching to investors. I went straight back to the crowdfunders.

I've now raised over £4 million for the company – and only 17% has been given out as shares.

A note on giving out shares... I've been invited onto *Dragons' Den* a number of times and always declined. I'm sure the PR from it would be wonderful, but it's a TV show, not a business forum. They give very little money away for a lot of equity in the pitchers' business.

Your company shares are your equity. Treat them well. Hold on to as many as you can without giving up on company growth. There's always a fine balance between the two, but when you do come to exit, you will be glad of this advice. I've known a lot of entrepreneurs who have accepted what they as perceived large investment sums for most of their company shares. Remember, investment into your company isn't money in your bank – but your shares are.

What crowdfunding gave MacRebur was not just money, but a crowd of people who had skin in the game, who were really interested in investing with us. We don't have anybody looking over our shoulder saying, 'You're doing the right thing' or 'You're doing the wrong thing'. Our investors are all from the crowd: family members and friends, and followers of an ecological environmental business. They are people who really support and trust us, and who are also helping by recommending us to everybody they know.

I've heard about businesses that give away 50% of their idea to high-end investors who are just there to make money. What I love about crowdfunding is that it isn't like that at all. It creates a group of supporters who put in as much money as they can afford and get some shares in the company in exchange. The business is funded through normal people, like you and me. People who want to make a difference.

Crowdfunding is a different way to raise money for good ideas. Entrepreneurs are increasingly bypassing more traditional funding routes such as bank loans or grants and turning instead to the people around them or in their community to support their ventures. The idea has been around for centuries, but the internet makes the potential audience huge.

A good friend of mine, Rob Love, is the founder of Crowdfunder UK, the UKs leading crowdfunding platform, which is based in Newquay, Cornwall. Rob explains that Crowdfunder UK projects come in all shapes and sizes. His company has helped more than 80,000 individuals, charities, businesses and community projects raise more than £100 million for their great ideas. That enables them to change lives and make an impact in their community. [11]

There are many examples of successful crowdfunding campaigns, including our own at MacRebur. We've raised over £4 million through crowdfunding, which has enabled us to build our business into a global brand.

Every day, more entrepreneurs are turning to crowdfunding to get their creative ideas and early-stage companies off the ground. The way that businesses find funding has fundamentally changed through a combination of rewards and equity crowdfunding, creating a win–win funding landscape. Crowdfunding backers can now own a piece of their favourite company through equity investment. Entrepreneurs can now convert their best customers and advocates into catalysts to move their business forwards.

There is no way to guarantee crowdfunding success, but you can maximise your chances by studying the projects, strategies and crowdfunding secrets that have worked for others. Like any other business venture, crowdfunding is a process that starts long before the doors are opened – and continues long after the campaign has closed.

Relationship with Money

So many new entrepreneurs have a funny relationship with money when they first start in business. I was coaching a client who had recently set up a business in nutrition and weight loss but her dis-ability was that she couldn't bring herself to charge for her weight-loss services. She had just finished creating a video tutorial series to help people lose weight and she was very proud of it. Although she was broke, she simply wasn't comfortable with charging money, so she was offering videos to people she knew for free.

I explained to her why I found this strange. Most of the products or services I buy are designed to save me time, which I see as my most valuable commodity. I'm happy to spend my money if I create more time in return. My challenge to her was that she was quite happy to take people's time to watch her videos, but she wouldn't take their money in exchange. If I want to lose weight, I want to learn how to do it now, not wait and spend more time not achieving my outcome while I'm waiting for her to get comfortable with taking my money.

As entrepreneurs, it's important to get comfortable with the concept of money.

Some people may have a *scarcity mindset*, as described by Steven Covey in his bestselling book *The 7 Habits of Highly Effective People.* With this mindset, you see money and other resources as zero-sum games, in which more for others means less for you, and vice versa.

With a scarcity mindset, you might feel bad whether the money is coming in or going out. Paying money to others feels bad because you see it as less money for you, but receiving money can make you feel guilty about 'taking' money from others.

Money is tied to basic survival for most of us, which is why we often attach feelings of fear to money.

Mindset Technique: Money Fears

Take some time to think about your relationship with money and how it was formed. Key questions you should ask yourself include:

- What's important to me about money?
- Where do my money values come from?
- How does money make me feel?
- Do I have a history with money?
- If I didn't have money, what is the worst thing that could happen?
- When I do have money, what happens next?
- Do I have any issues regarding money?
- Am I impulsive with money, or do I have the discipline to say no?
- How much money would I like to have?

If thinking about these questions makes you feel uncomfortable, you might not have a good relationship with money.

If you are looking for advice around money and your relationship with it, I have some resources on my website that I hope will help. **www.tobymccartney.com/businessReLOVEution**

Chapter 17 Principle:

Fund your business through means that allow you to do what you do: disrupt.

CHAPTER EIGHTEEN

Bloody Good Ideas

I HAVE BEEN LUCKY ENOUGH TO be selected to give three TEDx Talks, the first of which was at Cambridge University ('What if we talk rubbish?'). As a public speaker, giving a TEDx Talk has been one of the greatest opportunities of my life. It's a privilege to be asked to speak at all, but to be asked to speak about topics I'm passionate about is a bonus. I saw the value in what TEDx gave me as the opportunity to stand on a platform and present my message. I've gained a lot of clients through that experience.

BGi EVENTS

BLOODY GOOD IDEAS

Every year for 10 years, I applied to host a TEDx Talk in Carlisle, my home city. I wanted to give other people the chance to have their moment on stage and speak publicly about the ideas they're passionate about. Every year, I filled in the application forms – and every year, I was rejected. I read books about how to fill in the application forms. I even employed someone to fill them out for me, because I thought I wasn't doing it right. I always got the standard reply, 'Sorry, you have not been selected'. There was never any feedback as to why.

It was so frustrating not being given permission to host TED talks in Carlisle that Kate and I thought, *If they're not going to give us the chance, we'll just set it up ourselves*. So we launched BGI Talks, which provide a stage for anyone who has 'Bloody Good Ideas'. We hired venues with a stage, invited an audience and had it all filmed. The events have been very successful. As soon as we finished the first, people were inquiring about the next. And it all came from not getting permission to run a TEDx Talk in our local area.

In the UK, BGI Talks now take place in selected counties, organised through regional circuits. It is growing, but had not reached outside the UK before the COVID-19 crisis struck. Many people lost their jobs and businesses.

More than ever, people needed a platform to share their ideas. So we moved BGI Talks online. We book speakers and hire a team for filming, editing and getting the talks out there. For the first time, we run adverts for companies sponsoring the videos, which has given us a revenue stream we didn't have with live events. (That's an example, by the way, of seeing an opportunity in a crisis.)

Since starting BGI Talks, I have given two Tedx Talks of my own: TEDx Warwick ('Thinking in Green') and TEDx Chennai ('What if Plastic Made Roads'). At the latter, the second-largest TEDx stage in the world, there were nearly 5,000 people in the audience. The whole experience came full circle at the end of 2020, when we were finally granted the licence to host TEDx Carlisle.

The Law of Requisite Variety

In addition to my talks about plastic roads and the planet's waste plastic epidemic, Kate and I also give talks at conferences and universities about business skills and body language. We use these events to pitch our coaching services, mastermind groups and NLP training services – so without that public speaking platform, our businesses would not be as sustainable.

One thing the COVID-19 crisis taught everyone – especially business owners – is that we need to be open-minded. By letting go of preconceptions of how things are supposed to be, we open ourselves up to other available possibilities. And that means pivoting our business models.

The law of requisite variety comes from mathematics and physics. It says that the object with the most flexibility will always own the system. It's the same in business. A successful company has to have a set of procedures – but those procedures have to be flexible. Every client or every customer is going to be different, and so is every employee.

The whole premise of disrupting business for good is that we're going to bend the existing rules, which means we need to be flexible with our communication, flexible with our models, flexible with our procedures and our terms for everyone. That's the way we can ensure that we'll own the system rather than having our customers own the system.

The law of requisite variety is essential for any business. Take the pandemic and lockdowns. We took talks, coaching and training services that would normally be done live and turned them into remote events. We used the law of requisite variety. We moved our live training courses to Zoom and GoToMeeting and other platforms that allowed us to still be in a 'room' – just virtually.

Here are some more examples of businesses that successfully adapted during unprecedented times, disrupting the status quo for a greater good.

- To accommodate the COVID-19 crisis and social distancing measures, Piroshky Piroshky, a bakery in Seattle, Washington's iconic Pike Place Market, expanded their delivery services – but not just their own. The company's website was updated to include delivery options for other small businesses. It became so popular that dozens of businesses joined a waiting list to be included on the site – a service for which the bakery's owner, in the spirit of community, is not charging.

- Clothing brand Tultex redirected their production strategy to supply up to 2 million washable face masks per week, primarily for professionals in the healthcare industry. Tultex has had to adapt to nationwide needs before. During World War II, it switched production to making military uniforms.

Making the law of requisite variety key to our businesses means that we are flexible enough to adapt how we give our services to our customers. It means we can survive as a business, rather than potentially fail overnight.

The Flexible Mindset

I have always had what I like to call a 'Yes mindset', although it has sometimes been to my detriment. I tend to say 'Yes' to everything, then become comfortable with the consequences later.

A number of years ago Kate, who was frustrated with my entrepreneurial schemes, asked me to promise not to create any new businesses for a whole year. It was one of the most difficult years of my adult life. I had to say 'no' to so many things, but Kate was determined that I would put all my efforts into the businesses we had already established. I learned during that year that, while I have always been a great starter of things, I'm pretty poor at maintenance and completion. To be truly entrepreneurial and successful, I believe we need to develop new skills that sit outside our current mindset and be flexible with the mindset we do have.

Ross Ashby [12] a pioneering British cyberneticist and psychiatrist, formulated his law of requisite variety [13] in the context of regulation in biology, or how organisms are able to adapt to their environment. In his words: 'When the variety or complexity of the environment exceeds the capacity of a system (natural or artificial), the environment will dominate and ultimately destroy that system.'

I think entrepreneurs can adapt this law in business. If we all had the flexibility to deal appropriately with the range of challenges that the world throws at us, we would be able to choose from multiple solutions and would probably overcome many more problems.

With this in mind, I now actively look for problems facing the world today. I make sure that, for every problem I find, I come up with at least 10 solutions. No matter how ridiculous some of those solutions might be, I make sure that I am more flexible in my thoughts than the problem I am facing.

When I came up with the idea of putting waste plastics into roads, the solution came to me by looking at two world problems; on one side the poor quality of many roads, and on the other the waste plastic epidemic.

It was only by being flexible that I could come up with a simple way to combine both problems to find the ultimate solution.

 Exercise: Law of Requisite Variety

1. Think of a problem to which you haven't yet found a solution. Write down the problem on the left-hand side of a sheet of paper.
2. Apply the Law of Requisite Variety. Think up at least 10 crazy solutions to the problem and write them down on the right-hand side of the paper.

3. Now rank those solutions in order, from the easiest and most effective to implement to the hardest and least likely to succeed.

4. Phone your best friend and ask them for their feedback on the solutions you have come up with. Read out the problem, then read out the solutions ranked 1 to 10. Which do they think is best? Which do they dismiss? What suggestions do they make?

How many solutions do you now have to that problem you couldn't previously solve?

Chapter 18 Principle:

The business or person with the most flexibility will always own the system.

I'm Not as Fat as a Walrus

IN 2012, PAUL HAD FALLEN OUT WITH HIS FATHER AND THEIR RELATIONSHIP was at an all-time low. He had split up with his girlfriend of four years and was struggling because he missed her and wanted her back. He had become so pissed off with his job that he decided to leave. It was the first time in his life he had ever given up the security of having an income.

He had no idea what to do next. After an online search, he came along to a free weekend course Kate and I were running about NLP/ coaching/business skills. He learned some NLP tools and techniques and used them to overcome what he called a severe, 'in the bones', deep-rooted depression. The skills also helped him build a belief in himself that he could succeed in business and in life.

It's too complex to get into here, but Paul used Anchoring and Time-Based techniques (available through our programme 'The NLP Practitioner') to change his mindset. The thinking behind the techniques is that, if someone knows they feel depressed, then they must know and have access to how to feel differently. In order to feel depressed, we must also know what is not depressed...

Paul is now a professional public speaker. He works as a consul- tant for a number of charities. He is what is known as a major donor fundraiser. He and another participant he met in our programme have started a business running courses and training to coach clients through the type of depression Paul used to experience.

Paul isn't the only client we've had with such a story. One limiting belief that my wife and I often coach people through is that a participant doesn't feel they know enough in order to, for example, be a coach. They start an internal dialogue in which they tell themselves they don't have what it takes to confidently deal with new circumstances as they come up. One of the ways we challenge their thinking is to say, 'There are so many people out there that you could help, if only you could get over the selfish part of yourself that is unable to process your own fear.'

That usually works.

Chris Jones was a bit of a misfit. He couldn't stand up in a room and tell people his name because he was so inwardly focused. He was nervous, anxious and stressed. By learning some of the skills we teach in our programmes and applying the principles to his life, he was able to create a successful coaching business from his phobias. He now works alongside airlines, helping passengers overcome flying phobias. He's found his niche – or rather, his unicorn.

One of the things we've observed over the years is that many of our training participants have formed deep-rooted relationships as an outcome of participating in our programmes. So many business relationships emerge from the courses, and so many romantic relationships. We feel this is because of the way we approach business and the way we teach our clients to, first and foremost, be a friend.

To find out more about our programme, "The NLP Practitioner" and to delve deeper into the Anchoring and Time-Based Techniques, please visit:

www.tobymccartney.com/businessReLOVEution

Be Provocative (with Humour)

If you speak to somebody who can make you laugh about the ridiculous challenges that we all create for ourselves in our lives, you're 90% of the way towards shifting a mindset from one of sadness to one of joy.

Frank Farrelly is the founder of what's called Provocative Therapy. Frank would hold 20-minute long sessions – he called them interviews – with clients in which he would be provocative in order to provoke a response. The trick was, he used humour. Humour would prevent what he said from simply being perceived as rude.

When my wife and I went to see him – he has since died – we were in a group session where one woman went up to Frank and he asked her, 'What's your problem?' She said, 'I'm overweight.' He looked her square in the face and said, 'Oh, yeah, you're like a walrus.'

As an audience, we were all shocked; who could say that to somebody else? But in fact the woman then started to question her own challenge. She said, 'Well, no. I mean, I'm not *that* big. I'm just slightly overweight.' She then went on to share what she wanted to do about it. In other words, she started to re-analyse her statement. Frank followed up by explaining that his strategy was to provoke a response that causes someone to question whatever statement he or she had made. I was fascinated by this.

Since then, my wife and I have been willing to go beyond the traditional realms of therapy and ways of helping people by provoking a response that kicks them out of their current behaviours and moves them into behaviours that better serve them. Sometimes we need to be provocative with people – to bend the rules of therapy – to make a difference.

We ask the coaches in our programme how willing they are to help their clients break free from the behaviours and the mindset that they currently have. Are they willing to go all the way, to break rapport with their customers or their clients in order to get a response? Are *you* willing to challenge the beliefs you hold about yourself in this way?

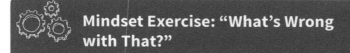

Mindset Exercise: "What's Wrong with That?"

1. Ask a friend to play the role of your therapist.
2. Pick a behaviour you want to change. Here the "therapist" emphasises the benefits of the client's dysfunctional behaviours and encourages them to do more of the same.
3. The more the client begins to protest that the therapist's suggestions may not actually be helping, the more the therapist insists that the client acts, thinks and feels the same.
4. The therapist will also wildly exaggerate the benefit of continuing in this manner and even offer 'instant research examples' to support this suggestion!

Be Provocative (with Purpose)

'If you want an audience, start a fight' – Irish proverb

The dictionary definition of provocative is 'causing a strong reaction, especially deliberately'. It's human nature to want to avoid causing annoyance, especially if it is irritating, awkward, uncomfortable or exasperating.[14] If you have read this far, you know that not only am I not afraid to be provocative, I quite enjoy it. But, with the caveat that it must have a purpose.

As John Kaufman points out in his book, *The Personal MBA: Master the Art of Business*, 'controversy with a purpose is valuable. A consistent level of mild controversy has allowed people to grow in their businesses, and [...] used constructively, controversy can be an effective way to attract attention. People start talking, engaging, and paying attention to your position, which is obviously a very good thing.'[15]

I would take it a step further and say that, in business, confrontation (and provocation) is absolutely necessary. Progress is often the result of disruption, and most people don't like to be disrupted. (A note of caution though, provocation will also attract the haters – but, remember: FUCM!)

I recently had my own opportunity to cause a ruckus. In the small village where I live in Scotland, the roads are a shocking state of disrepair. The second time I drove my new electric car, I hit a pothole and damaged a wheel, bursting the tyre. After spending a lot of money to fix it, I wrote to my local authority to complain. I don't often complain and would rather fix the problem myself, but on this occasion, I wanted to provide feedback and some solutions to the problems the local authority obviously have with regards to the lack of maintenance on our local roads. I got no response.

Every day, I drive both my daughters to school along that same potholed road and I didn't want my daughters to learn that I was just going to put up with a problem rather than do something about it.

One of the important parts of any business is to always look after your customers. My local authority seemed to have forgotten this, so I decided to continue.

I wrote another letter, sent an email, completed an online complaints form on their website – every week for 12 months.

No response. Nada.

Now the gloves were off. I believe that the meaning of your communication is the response you get. Because I got no response, I decided to change my communication. I filmed a three-minute video showing the state of the potholes on my local road and posted it on my social media sites, threatening to take further action unless they came and fixed the road within a seven-day period. The video went viral and was watched by nearly three thousand people on

Facebook alone. I also contacted a friend who works as a news-reader for a local TV news channel, got my PR team on board and sent out my story to see what response I would get. My TV friend asked me to gather some local residents to meet with a reporter the following day. I posted this to my social media posts. As if by magic, the local authority turned up the next morning, before the news reporter was due to arrive, and filled in all the potholes.

Of course, just six days later the potholes were back and so my saga to be provocative continues. But my point is that having an opinion or stating a position sets you apart from everyone else on the planet. For most people, it feels easier to do nothing – to put up with the potholes or hop on the bandwagon of public opinion – than to be a contrarian. But doing what everyone else does, and having everyone agree with you is boring. Not only that: no one will pay attention.

Always keep your eye on the bigger picture. Being provocative for its own sake can mean losing sight of your initial intention. If the ruckus you create has a purpose, and you're fully conscious of its effects on others, then it can be an effective tool to get people's attention. The more discussion you provoke, the more attention people pay, which will attract both supporters and benefactors. Sometimes – and especially if you are building a business that is designed to disrupt for good – you need to create a campaign that fights for your purpose. Be prepared to have unpopular opinions. Most people prefer to steer clear of being provocative, but as entre-preneurs sometimes we need to go in search of it.

Chapter 19 Principle:

Be provocative: Kick yourself out of behaviours that no longer serve you.

CHAPTER TWENTY

A Mile in Your Shoes

In 2012, I was invited to speak on behalf of Shelter, the homeless charity, at an event called The YES Group. The YES Group is an off-shoot of Tony Robbins programmes that typically feature coaches or other personal or business development guest speakers. This particular group met monthly in London, and I was speaking alongside a guy who had flown all the way from Australia to sell personal and professional development programmes.

My topic was the social aspect of homelessness, and how we can help others by disrupting business for good. I had a month to prepare my presentation, but I felt like a fraud. How could I speak about homelessness if I'd never been homeless? As an experiment, I decided to sleep rough for a while, as the homeless are forced to do.

I grew a beard and hired a makeup artist to make me look as if I'd been on the streets for ages. I put on clothes that were ripped and dirty and went out onto the streets of London. I took a film crew to follow me around. Just to ham it up a bit, I decided that I would sit outside the hotel where that month's YES Group meeting was about to be held.

The aim of the YES Group is to say, 'Yes, we'll help'. So I decided I would sit outside with a cardboard poster that read 'Please help'. I would then base my keynote presentation for the following month around what 'help' meant for the coaches and participants who are all there, in theory, to help.

I sat outside with a pinhole camera in the hoodie I was wearing, while the crew filmed me from behind a black sheet of glass in the hotel, where nobody could see them.

I got in position an hour before the meeting, so any attendees would have to walk past me. About 20 minutes before the meeting was due to start, the director drove up to the hotel in his new Jaguar – and walked straight past me.

Then some of the YES Group delegates started to arrive. One girl was wearing a T-shirt with the Gandhi quote 'Be the Change you want to see in the world'. As she walked past, she kicked me, spat at me and said, 'Get a fucking job'. A number of meeting attendees said the same thing, 'Get an effing job.' And I got them all on film.

As I sat there, the managers of the hotel asked me to move. They didn't want me sitting there. I moved around the corner, where I got a similar reaction from people as from the attendees of the YES group. But I remember one woman in particular who walked past me and then came back. She said, 'How long are you going to be here?' I thought she was going to throw a bucket of water over me or something, but I said, 'I'm here all the time.' She left but well over an hour later she came back with a £20 note. She gave it to me, saying, 'This is for you'.

I felt really guilty because I wasn't really on the streets. But I couldn't tell her that, so I took the money and I gave it to Shelter.

There was this huge contrast between the people who kicked, spat and swore, and told me to 'Get an effing job' and those who went out of their way to be overly kind and try to help me. I had people giving me McDonald's meals they had bought for me.

I slept on the streets that night. Of course, I always knew I had a credit card in my back pocket, so my experience wasn't all authentic, but I at least got a feeling for what it was like to be seen as a marginalised member of the community. London never sleeps, they say. Certainly, I didn't get any sleep because there were constantly people going back and forth. I was too nervous to sleep, anyway.

I just sat up all night, fascinated by the experience.

A month passed, and I was being introduced on stage in front of the YES Group to talk about charity and helping others. They greeted me with enthusiastic applause.

About five minutes in, I said, 'I understand that, as part of the YES group, you say yes to everything and want to help people. This talk is titled "What Help Really Means". Well, I filmed something about what people in this group think "help" means.'

I didn't want to judge their behaviour, but I was setting them up for a fall. It frustrated me so much that they said one thing but did another. My cardboard sign had said 'Please Help'. It didn't ask for food or money, just for help, in any way.

What does it really mean when someone asks for help? There was a lot of room for interpretation. My sign gave people an opportunity to say, 'How can I help?' But no-one from the YES Group had asked me that question.

From an entrepreneurial perspective, it's one of the first questions I ask. Entrepreneurs solve problems. It's not just a badge; it's how we build a business. And, in theory, members of the YES group are building businesses.

I played the video, and the audience watched themselves on film – kicking me, spitting at me, swearing at me – on their way into the YES Group meeting. The room went silent, but I continued with my speech. The rest of my speech was about what I believe 'help' to be. I was about to run the London Marathon for Shelter, so I spoke about how Shelter helps the homeless. I almost pretended that what I had just shown them hadn't happened, because I found that funnier than rubbing their faces in it. I didn't want to be the teacher in the room who told them off; I just wanted to say, 'This is the experience

I've had. You all decide what that means to you. I'm going to talk about Shelter.'

The organisers had asked me if I wanted to sell my products after the speech. I was representing a charity, so I didn't have anything to sell. The other speaker, on the other hand, was selling hard. I remember how one of his slides showed him with his top off, and he said, 'If you want to look like me, sign up for one of my courses'. His product tables had been set out hours before anyone arrived, filled with his books, CDs and videos all neatly arranged, with booking forms on hand and a team of people waiting to collect them.

After my talk, I had nothing on my table, but I sat there in case anyone had any questions. I thought no one would speak to me because they must all have hated me after secretly filming them and calling out their hypocrisy. In the end, there was no-one at the other speaker's table – it was very embarrassing for him – but a queue out of the door at my table.

People thanked me for the feedback and tried to talk about what I had done and what a unique approach it was. They absolutely loved the talk, even though they were shocked. (Well, not everyone loved the talk. The girl who had spat at me didn't come over!) But some of the others who were filmed were there. Some were really embarrassed and wanted to apologise, although I didn't need or ask for an apology. Others were really fascinated by what it was like to sleep rough, so they ignored their own behaviours and just took the message from the talk.

Strangely, I've never been invited back to the YES Group to speak again.

The main message I took from that experience is that people are not their behaviours. The people who behaved negatively towards me weren't necessarily bad people, it's just that their behaviours weren't great in that moment. Prisons are full of people with bad behaviours, but that doesn't make them all bad people.

I strongly believe that, if we work out who we are – if we identify our true identity and are faithful to it – then we can match our behaviours to ourselves. So many people take courses or learn new skills, and then identify themselves with those new skills. But those skills or that knowledge doesn't make them who they are. I think that's where we find incongruencies in people, when they try and match an identity with the behaviours that they have learned.

If we call ourselves a coach because we have learned coaching skills, that doesn't make us a coach. To be a coach, we have to be understanding and work towards helping others in whatever way possible.

We must de-identify with our behaviours, and instead identify with our true identity. Searching for our true identities is an ongoing challenge, but it's worth it. I used to call myself an entrepreneur, but then I realised that I'm not an entrepreneur with my wife, and I'm not an entrepreneur with my kids. Knowing that, I can get back on track to being the real me, rather than just being the behavioural me. Similarly, as I discussed earlier, I am not dyslexic, I just have some behaviours that can be labelled as characteristics of dyslexia. Having figured that out, I don't let 'having dyslexia' hold me back.

What I've worked out is that, with everyone—with my wife, my kids, my clients, customers, and new people I meet—I am consistently a friend. That is my true identity; now that I know that, friendly behaviour becomes natural to me.

 Mindset Exercises: The Seven Levels of Change

Our behaviours can change. There is a technique called Neurological Levels where we ask ourselves questions from seven different positions, or viewpoints. This technique has its foundations in the well-known Albert Einstein quote, 'We cannot solve our problems with the same thinking we used when we created them'. Here are the seven different positions:

Level One: Environment.

This covers every environmental consideration with regards to the problem or challenge. Ask yourself some basic questions at this level:

1. What can you keep within your environment?
2. What can you change within your environment?

A simple example would be if you are in an office and the environment isn't working for you – because it's too noisy or crowded, say, or because you're not getting any work done. What can you keep that does work and what can you change about what doesn't work?

During the COVID-19 lockdown, I completely transformed my office. Having worked in a main office with my employees, I started working from home. I had to turn the spare bedroom into an office. Now, when I work from that spare bedroom, rather than sitting on the bed and working on the laptop, I now feel more official, and that helps with my productivity and attentiveness.

Level Two: Behaviours.

1. What behaviours do you have that you wish to keep?
2. What behaviours do you wish to change in order to move closer to your goals?

Level Three: Skills.

1. What skills do you currently have that you wish to use more of?
2. What are the skills you don't have that you would like to gain, in order to help you move closer to that goal?

Level Four: Values.

1. What is important to you currently that you wish to use to move closer to your goal?

2. What values are not being met currently that you can go out to meet, which will help you move closer to your goal?

WHAT MOST PEOPLE WANT IN LIFE...
- respect
- equality
- growth
- belonging
- purpose

Level Five: Beliefs.

1. What beliefs do I currently hold that serve me?
2. What limiting beliefs don't serve me currently that I could replace with empowering beliefs that can help me move forwards?

Level Six: Identity.

Now that you've got all those things in place you discovered through the other levels, who are you? Who are you when the lights are on and when the lights are off? You are looking for that singular identity, the real person, the person you are when no one is around and no one is watching. When you fall outside of that real person, you find incongruency. What you are looking to do in your life, and in your business life, is to find congruency between all the different levels so that your behaviours match with who you call yourself.

To give you a negative example, imagine a therapist who can't wait for the cigarette break because he or she is addicted to nicotine. Well, if their therapy is to help people give up addictive behaviours, they are incongruent between their identity and their behaviours.

Look for that congruency, find out who you are and who you are to your customers, to your family, to your friends – who you are really when the lights are on and when the lights are off.

Level Seven: Purpose.

This is the place you think about that dash between your birth date and your death date, and what that dash is worth to you.

What does that dash represent to you?

1. What is your purpose on the planet and what is the overall purpose of the business?
2. Who are you serving?
3. How are you helping?
4. What are you disrupting? Remember, it's got to be disrupting for good: you want to make sure there is a real purpose and cause behind the disruption.

Those seven levels of thinking are useful when thinking about who you are and what the idea of being an entrepreneur is, so that you can get all seven levels matched up and aligned to becoming that real entrepreneur. That real 'you' that can move forwards with your business.

CHAPTER 20 Principle:

Behaviours can be changed.

Know When It's Time to Exit

SOMETHING I LEARNED RELATIVELY EARLY ON IN MY CAREER IS ONE OF THE most practical skills that's often overlooked: knowing when it's time to stop. Some of the businesses I have started – such as Capital Tutors or StayingLocal – could have become billion-pound businesses. I'll never know. Others could have turned into something completely different had I stuck with them. But I always know my limits.

I'm a start-up guy. I really enjoy coming up with a concept, setting a goal and building a business until it achieves that goal. My skill set does not go beyond that stage. Turning a business into a major corporation is not something I'm interested in achieving at this time.

I either shut the business down, sell it or franchise it.

BrainOBrain is the only business I have ever franchised (although we do offer licences to manufacture our products with MacRebur). BrainOBrain was another business that started through my experiences in India. It revolves around children using NLP. My wife and I had been using NLP with adults, but we had never worked out how to use it with kids. Since my learning style is so different from how many people learn, I have a real passion for teaching children who learn differently.

On a trip to India my wife and I became aware that some of the children we met in a school could learn to calculate using an abacus – a calculating tool made up of rods and balls – very quickly. We would ask, 'What's 34 multiplied by 251?' They would look at their fingers and give us the answer. In their mind, they were visualising an abacus, with its different rows of beads, and moving the beads to get the right answer. In other words, they were getting the answer visually, not working it out in the way we'd all been taught in school. I thought this was marvellous.

We decided to invest in a Master franchise licence from the company called BrainOBrain who taught these children in afterschools clubs and together with our NLP training combined them into a teaching method taught to children in the UK. My wife and I started to teach it at schools and realised that we were struggling by ourselves to really make an impact as we alone were too small for what the business needed to be. Everybody needed to know about these skills, not just the kids we could physically get in front of. So we franchised the business. We learned how to sell to teachers who wanted to buy into the franchise. They took teacher training through us, and then had their own region in which to teach. Once we'd done that, we sold BrainOBrain. It still operates all over the world as it is a fantastic afterschools club for kids who learn very differently.

That's another skill set entrepreneurs should have: knowing what needs to be done to scale a business up, and knowing what needs to be sold as is or closed down. It comes back to knowing what your skills are and when to exit. Traditional business advice may be to hire out the skill sets you don't have and carry on, keeping the business and scaling it.

My philosophy is different. If it's not just certain tasks that leave you uninspired, but the business itself, the traditional advice is of no use. Richard Branson once said, 'My number one rule *in* business, and *in* life, is to enjoy what you *do*…. If you don't enjoy what you are doing, then you shouldn't be doing it.'

It has to be fun. For us, what happened with BrainOBrain is that once we weren't teaching kids anymore, running the business came to be about selling franchises – which was not as much fun. Time to sell.

If I stayed in an unproductive role I wasn't enjoying, I would just be working within the business instead of working on growing the business. I am not against delegating. But I do tend to fire myself from a job every 90 days if I'm consistently doing the same thing over and over and not enjoying it – or if I'm simply not good at it.

Is It Done Yet?

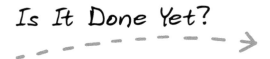

There is an Irish proverb that states, 'Well begun is half done'.

As a start-up guy, I love that saying. But while it may be true, half done is not the same as being completed. Recently, I stumbled across something known in the building and trades industry as the Law on Substantial Completion. I was intrigued. The most common definition of 'substantial completion' is the point in the project where a building can be used for its intended purpose. For example, in the typical building process, a property owner hires a contractor to complete a renovation. When the project nears completion, the owner often occupies the property and uses it even though the contractor has not yet finished the work he was contracted to complete. Nonetheless, the contractor asks for payment and provides warranties and other documentation, while continuing to finish up. The contractor's entitlement to payment will often depend on whether the contractor has reached "substantial completion".[16] What is interesting is that substantial completion is an odd concept that means "not quite done". [17] How this pertains to the modern entrepreneur is that it is only when we finish something – a task, a project, an idea – that the effort really matters. Ask my wife. I get excited by a new idea every single day. For many of us, completing tasks is the difficult bit. How many times has a task or project in your business been "substantially completed"?

This brings me to my next point about how to manage your time and energy. There comes a time in every entrepreneur's journey where they have to learn how to stay focused on what they are best at. Often, if you're anything like me, you enthusiastically start new projects or tasks but never complete them. You have to be aware how much of your time and energy these incomplete tasks are taking from progressing to the next phase in your business.

> 'Decide on your most important task. Begin immediately and work on that task with self-discipline until it is 100% complete. In life, all success comes from completing tasks. It's not from working at tasks, it's from completing tasks. It is only when you complete tasks that you become successful.'
>
> – BRIAN TRACY

There are only four ways to finish a task or project[18]:

- Complete It Now
- Stop Pretending You are Going to Complete it
- Hire Someone to Complete It
- Complete It Later

Complete It Now: Completing it now is the option most people think of first. If you keep a to-do list, you may assume that all those tasks are all your responsibility. But that's not quite true. This is the best option for important tasks that only you can do well – tasks that are the highest and best use of your time. Put differently, what is the 5% of your genius that only you can do, that nobody else does quite like you? This is your magic, your secret sauce.

Stop Pretending You are Going to Complete It: Eliminate the task. It's effective for anything that's unimportant or unnecessary. If it's not worth doing well or quickly, it's not worth doing at all. Don't hesitate to get rid of it.

Hire Someone to Complete It: Assign the task to someone else. Ninety percent of what you do can be handed off. This is the idea behind 'firing' yourself from a task every 90 days. If you're in the start-up stage where you're still figuring out your skill set, you might start by working within the business. When a task becomes something you're either not good at or not qualified to do, it's time to get somebody in that is going to do the job. Delegation is key. Employees, contractors, or outsources can all help you get the things done by completing the task on your behalf. *Upwork* and *Fiverr* make it possible to pass some tasks on that you're not good at, for not a great deal of money. If you feel like you can't afford to hire employees or contractors, your 'staff' could start out being a family member or a friend. I feel strongly that help is there when help is required.

Complete It Later: If the task is not crucial or time dependent, putting it off until later can be effective as long as it doesn't turn into a clever way to procrastinate. The best way to bog yourself down is by trying to handle too many things at once. Saving non-critical tasks for a future date is a good way to keep your attention and good energy focused on what's most important to you. In his book, *Getting Things Done*, David Allen recommends keeping a someday-maybe list of things that you'd like to do at some point, but that aren't important right now. Creativity researcher, Scott Belsky, recommends a similar approach in making ideas happen: create a back-burner list of tasks that you want to get to eventually, but that aren't a priority right now. Reviewing the list every few weeks is enough to identify tasks that you're ready to promote to active projects. You have to be careful that this doesn't turn into procrastination. Scheduling it in your calendar to be completed and then putting it out of your mind can also go a long way to giving you the space and energy to complete your essential and urgent tasks.

Each time you look at your to-do list, sort the things on it into these four options. You'll find that the number of things you tick off it will go shooting up.

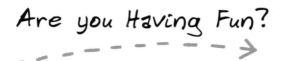

Are you Having Fun?

At the time of writing this, I am about to embark on another round of funding for MacRebur. I know that the first question I will be asked is 'What do you think your company is worth?' The second will be 'What is your exit strategy?' From their perspective, investors want to know, 'If I put in £1 million today, what will I pull out when these guys exit, and how soon will that be?'

These are the wrong questions!

I understand that business is business, but if I was investing in a company, I would be far more interested in the passion the team has for that business. And I would hope that they wouldn't be focused on an exit, but how big they can make the company and how much they can disrupt.

There weren't many people who saw the last financial depression coming and no-one imagined the shitstorm that COVID-19 brought to the world, so to ask any CEO how and when they plan to exit is like asking people what the weather will be like next Christmas. The truth is, we just don't know. As much as we can plan, we never know what is around the corner.

Richard Branson asked me that same question, 'What's your exit strategy?' I gave him my canned response and he simply looked at me and said, 'Wrong answer. The right answer is "You exit when it's not fun anymore"'. I learnt a valuable lesson that day.

You've got to do things that you love: the things that make you get up in the morning and think, 'God, I can't wait to do that.' Some people let the fear of failure slow them down or get in the way or stop them from pursuing their vision, especially if they don't yet identify themselves as an entrepreneur. Some of you might think, 'I'm just an employee' or 'I'm a manager,' or 'I don't have that skill set'.

Starting a business can be intimidating. My philosophy is to give your passion a go – see what happens. But have an outcome planned – know what you would like to have happen. Otherwise you're just running with it and hoping, and as far as I know there's no business built on hope alone.

Failure just means that the outcome you have is different from the outcome you intended. It doesn't mean you didn't gain something valuable and worthwhile.

Chapter 21 Principle:

When you stop having fun,
stop doing it.

Break Free

MAHATMA GANDHI IS KNOWN WORLDWIDE FOR LEADING A NONVIOLENT RESIS-tance campaign that eventually led to India's independence from British rule. On one especially busy day, Gandhi's advisors told him they had a very busy schedule, with twice as much to do as usual. Could he skip morning meditation and get to work? Gandhi replied that if they had twice as much work to do, they had better meditate for twice as long.

First of all, if you've made it this far through my book, congrat-ulations. Thank you for giving my words your most valuable com-modity: time.

You likely picked up this book because you have been doing the same thing over and over again and you are looking for something new for yourself. You realise you are worth more than whatever you are doing right now and you came to this book looking for alterna-tives to the mundane. You want to break free. You have a purpose in the world that you want to fulfill. You have the passion; and now you have all the mindset strategies and tools to do that. The next step is to turn it into day-to-day work.

If you have made it this far, you probably fit into one of three categories: overwhelmed, excited or curious.

Overwhelmed. If you are completely overwhelmed with the changes you are making in your life to accommodate your business and are finding it hard to focus on any one thing you have read, I encourage you to take Gandhi's lead. Focus on turning inwards, first, before moving outwards. Not just because it's healthy, but because it's essential to doing good, creative work. There's something to be said about the correct order of things. Without a strong connection inwards, our work in the world can never expand into its full potential. Nothing truly great has ever come out of stress. It's as simple as that. I recommend taking the next hour to read back through the book, and then practice the 'sanctuary' and 'purple liquid' meditation. Cancel any appointments you have until you can find your sanctuary and you have listened to my 'purple liquid' audio which can be found on my website: www.tobymccartney.com/businessReLOVEution

Excited. If you're feeling excited about getting started, I know you already understand that you have to work on your own mindset before you will see any success in your personal and business life. Becoming a modern entrepreneur is not an easy task, but if you are willing to put the exercises in this book into practice, you will start to see better results in your life and those results will, without any doubt, spread into your businesses. Go forward and seize the day: *carpe diem*. Look through a new lens for the opportunities that await you – they are out there – and know that you can continue to add more and more mindset techniques from this book into your life and your business.

Curious. If you realise that you need some help and support to truly make a success of your business and you're curious about what support is available, please contact me. If you are the right person for my training programmes, mastermind groups, membership organisations or mentoring programmes, I can work wonders for you. But you have to be the right fit. The first step to finding out is to visit my website and book a clarity call with me and my team and let's work out how we can work together. We will setup a call and talk you through the opportunities available to you.

www.tobymccartney.com/businessReLOVEution

Alternatively, send an email to **support@tobymccartney.com**, say you're interested in working with us and we will send you further information in response to your email.

This entire book was written to encourage you to embrace the modern entrepreneur within you. Hopefully it has given you the freedom you need to succeed. You have got nothing to lose. Take the mindset strategies I use in this book to disrupt your industry for good.

Acknowledgments

I'D LOVE TO THANK...

My wife, Kate and my children, India and Keira, because you are my everything and you love me despite my madness. We will always walk hand-in-hand together through everything life throws at us.

To my Dad who taught me how to have a sense of humour; an essential life skill so many are missing.

To my Mum who put up with me and my occasional acts of lunacy.

To my mother-in-law, Janice and father-in-law, Alan, who have always supported my wife and me in our many crazy schemes, and are always there with guidance and love.

My Grandfather who built my tuckbox and whose beer and cigars I stole and sold at school.

My business partners Gordon Reid and Nick Burnett for trusting me just enough to journey with me in business, while still maintaining our good friendship even in the most challenging times.

Emma Bulmer for managing me and putting up with my B.S.

My whole family at MacRebur, for helping us turn our ideas into reality.

Sir Richard Branson for inspiring me from such an early age and for making the decision to make me a winner.

James Timpson for inspiring me to maintain strong ethics in my businesses.

Rob Love for being a friend and for all of your support and belief in MacRebur.

Topher Morrison for being a friend and for your mentorship.

About the

Author

TOBY MCCARTNEY WAS BORN into a British army family in 1977 in North Yorkshire and attended a boarding school from a young age in Cumbria, UK. Although Toby left school at 18 without any qualifications, he discovered a real interest in business from an early age.

Toby's businesses and projects range from setting up one of the first ever internet hotel advertising platforms to creating char-

ities like Tobysshoes.com and GivingAfrica.org. He managed and produced a number one selling album with a band (FionaClayton.com), and ran a training company providing programs for children (Brainobrain.com), and still runs courses and workshops across the world for adults in NLP and Coaching, as well as public speaking and train the trainer programmes (tobyandkatemccartney.com) and the internationally acclaimed "Plastic Roads Company" (mac-rebur.com). He has written his own book on *Mastering Memory* and co-authored a book with his wife called *The NLP Practitioner*. Toby has won many awards, from Richard Branson's Virgin VOOM 2016 Award, to IoD's Director of the year, business and entrepreneur awards to innovation and education — Toby's career is dedicated to entrepreneurialism.

As Toby continues to grow as an entrepreneur and business leader, he is keen to share his experiences, knowledge and skills with as many budding entrepreneurs and potential leaders as possible, either through his training programmes or with his one-to-one business coaching sessions

He is an advocate of combining both life purpose with profit and believes these two are powerful motivators for change in the world. Toby has been happily married to his wife, Kate, for 19 years and counting – and they are proud parents of two little girls, India and Keira. They live in rural Scotland with their two dogs, two cats, goats and a free pub in their back garden.

If it's not fun, don't bother doing it!

Notes

1 https://www.amanet.org/articles/new-research-reveals-many-entrepreneurs-are-dyslexic/

2 https://socialinnovationexchange.org/insights/25-companies-carrying-out-corporate-social-innovation

3 https://digitalmarketinginstitute.com/en-gb/blog/corporate-16-brands-doing-corporate-social-responsibility-successfully

4 https://www.investopedia.com/articles/personal-finance/032415/why-are-tesla-cars-so-expensive.asp

5 https://www.warbyparker.com/history

6 https://www.bloomberg.com/news/features/2020-07-22/how-ben-jerry-s-applied-its-corporate-activism-recipe-to-blm

7 https://www.benjerry.com/about-us/media-center/dismantle-white-supremacy

8 https://www.subscriptioninsider.com/monetization/auto-renew-subscription/peloton-reports-triple-digit-increases-in-q4-fy-2020-fitness-subscriptions-and-revenue

9 The Journal of Marketing Theory and Practice, Quesenberry and research partner Michael Coolsen

10 https://www.wrvo.org/post/neuroscience-shows-brain-wired-story#stream/0

11 https://urldefense.proofpoint.com/v2/url?u=https-3A__wavelengthmag.com_inspired-2Dsurfer-2Drob-2Dlove_&d=DwIDaQ&c=euGZstcaTDllvimEN8b7jXrwqOf-v5A_CdpgnVfiiMM&r=_en43xNiLkQwdczEqxv2s5a4g2jXtlDibNtHOV19WqQ&m=zWSr3TsQXjfci53sNqKcaeKiZFXyo4YT17CnVIXllyE&s=_M_3pg3Q7e9OlGYBFDfIF1WJ-U6WSyBMzndYml36XFQ&e=

https://www.crowdfunder.co.uk/

12 http://www.rossashby.info

13 http://pespmc1.vub.ac.be/REQVAR.html

14 https://www.inc.com/marcel-schwantes/want-to-talk-with-more-confidence-try-the-1-thing-most-people-are-terrified-of.html

15 https://personalmba.com/controversy/

16 https://www.natlawreview.com/article/what-substantial-completion-and-why-it-important

17 https://www.ecmag.com/section/your-business/it-done-yet-law-substantial-completion

18 https://personalmba.com/4-methods-of-completion/

Lightning Source UK Ltd.
Milton Keynes UK
UKHW021123150421
382040UK00013B/1046